Merrell's Strong Start—Pre-K

A Social & Emotional Learning Curriculum

Second Edition

by

Sara A. Whitcomb, Ph.D.
University of Massachusetts
Amherst

and

Danielle M. Parisi Damico, Ph.D.
Amplify Education, Inc.
Brooklyn, New York

·P·A·U·L·H·
BROOKES
PUBLISHING C°®

Baltimore • London • Sydney

Paul H. Brookes Publishing Co.
Post Office Box 10624
Baltimore, Maryland 21285-0624
USA

www.brookespublishing.com

Typeset by Absolute Service, Inc., Towson, Maryland.
Manufactured in the United States of America by
Sheridan Books, Inc., Chelsea, Michigan.

The individuals described in this book are composites or real people whose situations are masked and are based on the authors' experiences. In all instances, names and identifying details have been changed to protect confidentiality.

Cover image © istockphoto/emholk
Stock photos and clip art are © istockphoto.com and Jupiterimages Corporation.

Source for Chapter 1 extract: From "Enhancing school-based prevention and youth development through coordinated social, emotional, and academic learning," by M.T. Greenberg, et al., *American Psychologist,* 2003, 58, pp. 466–474.

"If you're sad and you know it, say 'Boo hoo'." From *Activities for Responsive Caregiving: Infants, Toddlers, and Twos* by Jean Barbre. Copyright © 2013 by Jean Barbre. Reprinted with permission of Redleaf Press, St. Paul, MN; www.redleafpress.org.

Library of Congress Cataloging-in-Publication Data

The Library of Congress has cataloged the print edition as follows:

Names: Whitcomb, Sara A., author. | Parisi Damico, Danielle M., author. | Merrell, Kenneth W. Strong start, pre-K.
Title: Merrell's strong start, pre-K : a social and emotional learning curriculum / Sara A. Whitcomb, Ph.D., University of Massachusetts, Amherst and Danielle M. Parisi Damico, Ph.D., Amplify Education, Brooklyn, New York.
Description: Second edition. | Baltimore, Maryland : Brookes Publishing, 2016. | Series: Strong kids | Revised edition of: Strong start, pre-K / Kenneth W. Merrell, Sara A. Whitcomb, and Danielle M. Parisi. c2009. | Includes bibliographical references and index.
Identifiers: LCCN 2015038131 | ISBN 9781598579697 (paperback)
Subjects: LCSH: Affective education. | Early childhood education. | Social learning. | Child development | Emotional intelligence. | Education–Social aspects. | BISAC: EDUCATION / Preschool & Kindergarten.
Classification: LCC LB1072 .W55 2016 | DDC 370.15/34–dc23 LC record available at http://lccn.loc.gov/2015038131

British Library Cataloguing in Publication data are available from the British Library.

2020   2019   2018   2017   2016

10   9   8   7   6   5   4   3   2   1

Merrell's Strong Start—Pre-K

Second Edition

 **STRONG KIDS**™

Other programs in **Strong Kids™:**
A Social & Emotional Learning Curriculum

Merrell's Strong Start—Grades K–2:
A Social & Emotional Learning Curriculum,
Second Edition

Merrell's Strong Kids—Grades 3–5:
A Social & Emotional Learning Curriculum,
Second Edition

Merrell's Strong Kids—Grades 6–8:
A Social & Emotional Learning Curriculum,
Second Edition

Merrell's Strong Teens—Grades 9–12:
A Social & Emotional Learning Curriculum,
Second Edition

Contents

About the Downloadable Material

Purchasers of this book may download, print, and/or photocopy the ancillary material for educational use. These materials are included with the print book and are also available at www.brookespublishing.com/downloads, keycode: 26ctRaM9p

CONTENTS OF THE DOWNLOADABLE MATERIAL

Lesson 1

Supplement 1.1: About *Strong Start*
Strong Start Bulletin
Fidelity Checklist

Lesson 2

Supplement 2.1: Basic Feelings: Happy
Supplement 2.2: Basic Feelings: Sad
Supplement 2.3: Basic Feelings: Afraid
Supplement 2.4: Basic Feelings: Angry
Supplement 2.5: Basic Feelings: Surprised
Supplement 2.6: Basic Feelings: Disgusted
Supplement 2.7: Basic Feelings
Strong Start Bulletin
Fidelity Checklist

Lesson 3

Supplement 3.1: Basic Feelings: Happy
Supplement 3.2: Basic Feelings: Sad
Supplement 3.3: Basic Feelings: Afraid
Supplement 3.4: Basic Feelings: Angry
Supplement 3.5: Basic Feelings: Surprised
Supplement 3.6: Basic Feelings: Disgusted
Supplement 3.7: Feelings Bubbles
Strong Start Bulletin
Fidelity Checklist

Lesson 4

Supplement 4.1: Basic Feelings: Happy
Supplement 4.2: Basic Feelings: Sad
Supplement 4.3: Basic Feelings: Afraid
Supplement 4.4: Basic Feelings: Angry
Supplement 4.5: Basic Feelings: Surprised
Supplement 4.6: Basic Feelings: Disgusted
Strong Start Bulletin
Fidelity Checklist

Lesson 5

Supplement 5.1: I'm Angry!
Supplement 5.2: Basic Feelings: Angry
Supplement 5.3: The Stop, Count, In, Out Strategy
Supplement 5.4: Stop Sign
Strong Start Bulletin
Fidelity Checklist

Lesson 6

Supplement 6.1: I'm Happy!
Supplement 6.2: Basic Feelings: Happy
Strong Start Bulletin
Fidelity Checklist

Lesson 7

Supplement 7.1: I'm Worried!
Supplement 7.2: The Stop, Count, In, Out Strategy
Strong Start Bulletin
Fidelity Checklist

Lesson 8

Supplement 8.1: What Does a Good Friend Do?
Strong Start Bulletin
Fidelity Checklist

Lesson 9

Supplement 9.1: The Stop, Count, In, Out Strategy
Strong Start Bulletin
Fidelity Checklist

Lesson 10

Supplement 10.1: About *Strong Start*
Supplement 10.2: Basic Feelings
Supplement 10.3: The Stop, Count, In, Out Strategy
Strong Start Bulletin
Fidelity Checklist

Appendix A

Supplement A.1: Basic Feelings Cards
Supplement A.2: *Strong Start* Feelings Bingo
Supplement A.3: Bingo Spinner

About the Authors

Sara A. Whitcomb, Ph.D., Associate Professor, School Psychology, Department of Student Development, University of Massachusetts, Amherst, 111 Thatcher Way, Hills House South, Amherst, Massachusetts 01003

Dr. Whitcomb is Associate Professor in the School Psychology program in the Department of Student Development at the University of Massachusetts in Amherst. She teaches courses pertaining to developmental psychopathology, psychology in the classroom, behavioral assessment, and school-based consultation. Dr. Whitcomb works with several school districts on their implementation of schoolwide positive behavior interventions and support, and her current research efforts include investigation of quality implementation features and consultation related to school-based behavioral and social-emotional learning efforts. She has coauthored several articles and (with Kenneth W. Merrell) the fourth edition of a textbook entitled *Behavioral, Social, and Emotional Assessment for Children and Adolescents* (Routledge, 2013). She previously held positions as a special education and general education teacher in Grades K–8.

Danielle M. Parisi Damico, Ph.D., Research Scientist, Amplify Education, Inc., 55 Washington Street, Suite 900, Brooklyn, New York 11201

Dr. Parisi Damico is Research Scientist with Amplify, an educational technology company. She is a school psychologist whose work emphasizes prevention and early intervention for improving academic and social outcomes for students. She conducts research and provides professional development in the areas of response to intervention/multi-tiered systems of support, evidence-based instructional practices, and data-based decision making.

Foreword

This remarkable curricular program is a fitting tribute to Ken Merrell's legacy as one of the foremost scholar–innovators in the realm of emotional literacy and social and emotional learning (SEL). This work, along with its authors, are clearly reflective of the superb contributions that Ken made to our field of practice and research inquiry in teaching our school-age students, from preschool through high school, how to manage their emotions and attitudes in a healthier, more competent manner. I am honored to write this foreword as a means of acknowledging the work that Ken contributed and inspired in a career that was cut short so tragically.

Children and youth today are exposed constantly to so much toxicity in our national discourse about all manner of societal issues, not to mention the potential abuses of pervasive social media use that so dominates their lives. We do not provide them with competent models of interpersonal behavior nor with the tools for evaluating and making sense of what they hear and see. Nor do we model and teach healthy strategies for problem solving difficult social and interpersonal situations. Far too many youth today do not have the means to access material such as that provided in the *Strong Kids*™ curriculum. I can think of no other current innovation deliverable within the schooling context that holds greater importance for our youth's future than this one.

Mastery of the content of this curricular program has so many uses in a student's daily life that are manifested in one's self-management as well as in relating to others. This content holds substantial potential for improving student mental health and social relationships throughout one's social network. This program revision introduces "emotion identification" that allows students to better cope with complex and concurrent emotions, and students are taught how to confront their emotions in a proactive manner rather than as something to simply change or fix. Students are taught about emotional expression in contextual terms that include not only how they are expressed but with whom and where. The scenarios provided as teaching aids are authentic and carefully referenced to the problems and social situations today's students are likely to experience within their respective social networks. In terms of useful content, there seems to be very little that the authors have overlooked. I am especially impressed with the material on selecting smart, achievable goals and strategies for integrating SEL content across social settings and the generalizability–sustainability of key concepts.

The new content added to this revision passes the logic test for me in that it encompasses exactly what I think students of today need to cope effectively with the challenges and stresses of their daily life. These include units on understanding your emotions, understanding the emotions of others, dealing with anger, clear thinking, solving people problems, letting go of stress, positive living, behavior change, and finishing UP. These essential competencies are embedded within five lessons focused respectively on self-awareness, self-management, social awareness, relationship skills, and responsible decision-making. Exposure to and mastery of this material through a universal curricular teaching approach would go a long way toward enhancing the socialization process for many of our stressed out and anxious students. I am also impressed with the section on mindfulness and frankly did not expect such a unit in a curriculum of this type. However, as the authors present it, this material appears to fit seamlessly with the other content.

I have long believed that best practices in the SEL domain involve use of the most effective principles of academic instruction to teach this content. There are two types of mastery that should be addressed in this regard: *conceptual and behavioral*. This curriculum addresses both types of mastery and also provides for the universal and small group/individualized teaching of the content for those students who struggle with mastery in a group context. I applaud the authors for their accommodation of this important task in their work.

Over 20 years of research and development have been invested in this program to date. It is also grounded in a strong practitioner feedback loop that has provided invaluable information on the best ways to teach this content in a user-friendly fashion that students find appealing and acceptable. More than anything I can think of, the *Strong Kids* curriculum holds the potential to realize schools' role in promoting the emotional literacy and mental health of today's students. The *Strong Kids* curriculum program is very well designed, meets the best standards of curricular development, is easy to teach, and—best of all—students seem to like it, which, in my view, is the ultimate test of such a product. The *Strong Kids* curriculum is indeed a seminal contribution to our knowledge and practice base on social-emotional development. We owe Ken Merrell and the authors a huge debt!

Hill M. Walker, Ph.D.
Professor Emeritus
College of Education
University of Oregon

Acknowledgments

We would like to take this opportunity to express our gratitude for so many people who have been incredibly helpful in the preparation of the second edition of *Strong Start—Pre-K* and *Strong Start—Grades K–2*. First, we want to recognize the amazing contributions of graduate students Laura Linck and Kate Perkins. Both are former elementary school teachers who shared their insights and creative ideas to improve these curricula. They offered new, innovative ideas for *Strong Start* activities and children's literature. We would like to thank all of the individuals at Paul H. Brookes Publishing Co. who have supported us and believe in the utility of the Strong Kids™ series—Johanna Schmitter, Sarah Zerofsky, and Rebecca Lazo, among many others.

Finally, these curricula would not exist without the wisdom and guidance of our late mentor, Kenneth W. Merrell. Ken helped us to understand that social and emotional competencies could be systematically taught and that schools embracing this paradigm are likely to have happier students and teachers. We are so thankful that he gave us the opportunity to coauthor the first editions of *Strong Start*, and we know that his legacy lives on in many, including all the schools that have used *Strong Kids*, the researchers who further his work, and the graduate students at the University of Oregon who are honored with the annual Kenneth W. Merrell Legacy Scholarship.

Introduction and Overview

CHAPTER 1

About *Strong Start*

Strong Kids™: A Social and Emotional Learning Curriculum consists of five brief and practical social and emotional learning (SEL) programs that have been designed for the purpose of promoting the SEL of children in prekindergarten through 12th grade. *Strong Start—Pre-K*, the first volume in the Strong Kids curriculum, is for children in preschool (or approximately ages 3–5). *Strong Start* is designed to be both a prevention and an early intervention (EI) program, and it has a wide range of applications with high-functioning or typically developing children or with children who have learning or behavioral challenges. It can be used in a variety of settings.

We view *Strong Start* as a carefully designed SEL program intended to prevent the development of certain mental health problems and promote social and emotional wellness among young children. Moreover, we created this curriculum as a companion to the proven *Strong Start—Grades K–2, Strong Kids—Grades 3–5, Strong Kids—Grades 6–8,* and *Strong Teens—Grades 9–12* programs, which are largely cognitive-behavioral in nature and were designed for use with older children and adolescents. *Strong Start* is not the right program for *all* problems or purposes. The overall goals and objectives of the lessons focus on helping young students build awareness of their emotions and the emotions of others as well as create strategies for managing emotions in healthy ways.

Strong Start is a low-cost, low-technology program that can be implemented in a school or related educational setting. It is not necessary to be a licensed mental health professional in order to learn and implement this curriculum. The curriculum also can be taught in a self-contained manner within a specific environment and does not require expensive community wraparound services or mandatory parent training groups. The advantage of this programming approach is that *Strong Start* is brief, efficient, skill based, portable, and focused.

There are several appropriate settings for use of this curriculum, including, but not limited to, public preschool settings, private preschool settings, Head Start, and early childhood facilities that have an educational component. A wide range of professionals may appropriately serve as group leaders or instructors for this curriculum: general and special education teachers, speech-language pathologists, school counselors, social workers, psychologists, early interventionists, and other education or mental health professionals.

PROMOTING CHILDREN'S MENTAL HEALTH

The primary mission of schools traditionally has been viewed as promoting the development of academic skills, but there is no question that most educators, parents, and the general public support and expect a broader mission for schools. Greenberg and his colleagues stated

> High-quality education should teach young people to interact in socially skilled and respectful ways; to practice positive, safe, and healthy behaviors; to contribute ethically and responsibly to their peer group, family, school, and community; and to possess basic competencies, work habits, and values as a foundation for meaningful employment and citizenship....We consequently assert that school-based prevention programming—based on coordinated social, emotional, and academic learning—should be fundamental to preschool through high school education. (2003, pp. 466–467)

We agree with this statement. We also propose that teaching children positive social, emotional, and behavioral skills is a critical challenge facing our society. Changes in the structure of society and families have resulted in an increasing percentage of children and families who are at risk for developing a variety of behavioral, social, and mental health problems (e.g., Weissberg, Walberg, O'Brien, & Kuster, 2003). Greenberg, Domitrovich, and Bumbarger (2001) stated that between 12% and 22% of children and adolescents younger than age 18 experience mental health problems of sufficient severity to be in need of services. Educators are faced with working with these populations while also managing pressures from accountability efforts, schoolwide reform, increasing class sizes, and shrinking budgets.

Despite sincere and well-meaning attempts to offer real solutions to the social, emotional, and mental health problems of students in school settings, many of the programs or interventions that have been implemented are simply ineffective, inefficient, or fragmented. Despite these problems and challenges, there is reason for optimism regarding our ability to positively affect the social and emotional health and resilience of children, even those from very adverse life circumstances. One reason for this optimism is the accumulation of a large body of scientific evidence regarding what has been termed *developmental resilience* (Doll & Lyon, 1998). This notion concerns the ability of individuals to cope successfully with adversity, risk factors, and severe life stress and for young people to develop into competent and happy adults despite these problems.

Central to this notion of developmental resilience is the idea that some characteristics of resilience—the cognitive, behavioral, and affective skills that enable one to cope effectively with adversity—may be systematically taught and learned. Although some aspects of resilience or developmental hardiness may be innate or biologically based, evidence shows that learning plays a crucial role in developing the ability to cope effectively with problems and challenges. Stated simply, the ability to be resilient and to cope effectively in the face of adverse circumstances and challenges in life is something that can be acquired in great measure through systematic and effective instruction in the critical requisite skills involved.

SOCIAL AND EMOTIONAL LEARNING

Another reason for optimism regarding our ability to positively affect the social and emotional health and resilience of children is the evidence in the area of SEL (Zins, Bloodworth, Weissberg, & Walberg, 2004). SEL has been defined as systematic, cohesive, and effective instructional programming designed to teach social and emotional skills to children and adolescents, to prevent mental health problems, and to provide effective EI for those problems that are beginning to emerge (Greenberg et al., 2003). There are many manifestations of SEL programs, ranging from simple training in social or other life skills to expansive, multipronged efforts to prevent antisocial behavior and conduct problems. Since about the early 1990s, an impressive array of evidence-based SEL programs has been developed and made available for use in education and mental health. These programs vary substantially in mode of instruction, time and resources required, and cost, but they typically target internal developmental assets such as self-awareness, self-management, social awareness, relationship skills, and responsible decision making (Collaborative for Academic, Social, and Emotional Learning [CASEL], 2012). An analysis published by Durlak, Weissberg, Dymnicki, Taylor, and Schellinger (2011) suggested that SAFE programs are effective. SAFE programs are those that are *sequenced, active, focused,* and *explicit*. This analysis included a review of 213 studies of universal SEL interventions for children in preschool through 12th grade. Study outcomes consistently suggested statistically significant improvements in social-emotional skills, socially appropriate behavior, positive attitudes, and academic performance. In addition, statistically significant decreases were found in conduct problems and emotional distress.

The specific type of SEL program selected will depend on the specific needs and requirements of an institution or community and the competencies and problems that are most important to target, but those efforts that are most successful tend to be implemented in a planned, cohesive manner within a system. Fragmented, uncoordinated efforts seldom produce more than superficial, short-term results. Emory Cowen (1994), a pioneer in the modern science of mental health and wellness promotion, has argued that there are five main pathways to wellness:

1. Forming wholesome early attachments

2. Acquiring age-appropriate competencies

3. Being exposed to settings that favor wellness outcomes

4. Having the empowering sense of being in control of one's fate

5. Coping effectively with stress

It stands to reason, then, that for optimal effectiveness and impact, any comprehensive SEL program should address most, if not all, of these critical pathways.

SOCIAL AND EMOTIONAL NEEDS OF PRESCHOOL CHILDREN

To be effective, a curriculum must be designed and implemented to be developmentally appropriate for the students for whom it is intended. For preschool children, there are some unique cognitive, social, and emotional developmental needs that must be considered. Cognitively, children in this age range are *concrete thinkers*, meaning that they have not yet developed the ability to think abstractly or symbolically. They usually have difficulty with tasks that require a great deal of interpersonal insight or self-reflection. In addition, most preschool children have not yet learned to read. Therefore, any curriculum designed for this age group must be explicit and somewhat concrete, use examples with which the children are familiar, use repetition and review to help teach mastery of skills, require no reading skills, and be short enough and interesting enough to maintain their attention.

Children in preschool are developing emotionally and experiencing many emotional changes. They experience many feelings and tend to understand the general notion of feelings or emotions, but they usually have a very limited vocabulary of words to describe different emotions. For example, most preschool children will understand the concepts of *happy, sad,* and *mad,* but they may be less likely to know more sophisticated emotional words such as *worried, thrilled, joyful, tense,* or *proud.* Some of the critical tasks for children in this age range, in terms of emotional development, include developing a sense of self-control, learning new emotional words, learning that what is "right" or "wrong" may be based on more than just the immediate consequences of the behavior, and learning that how something appears is not always how it is.

Socially, preschool children are learning how to initiate effective social interactions with other children and how to develop friendships. They are in the process of learning how to engage socially with individuals outside of their family. Some of the critical skills during this period include learning to negotiate and compromise, learning to be empathetic or understand the feelings and experiences of another person, and learning how to effectively join groups and initiate conversations. Many of the friendships children develop at this age are not lasting, but they tend to be very important in terms of providing a situation in which children can learn the skills required to make friends and to be a good friend to others. Children who fail to acquire the empathy or social skills needed to be successful in making and keeping friends are at risk for a variety of social and emotional problems, ranging from isolation and peer rejection to loneliness, poor self-esteem, and even depression.

In sum, any SEL program designed for use with preschool children must take into account the unique developmental needs of this age group if it is to be effective. The developmental needs that must be considered include cognitive, emotional, and social development, among other issues.

MODEL FOR PREVENTING BEHAVIORAL AND EMOTIONAL PROBLEMS

Educational researchers have adapted a public health prevention model for use in school systems (e.g., Merrell & Buchanan, 2006; U.S. Department of Education,

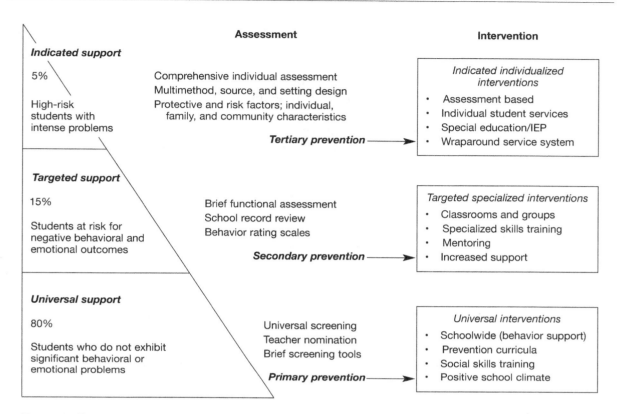

Figure 1.1. The prevention triangle model, specifically adapted for how to make systems work for assessing, identifying, and serving students with behavioral, social, and emotional problems. (*Key:* IEP, individualized education program.)

2004; Walker et al., 1996). We believe that this model (see Figure 1.1) has great importance for promoting SEL and for school-based promotion of children's mental health in general. Sometimes referred to as the "triangle," this model of prevention and intervention includes service delivery at three levels of prevention: students who currently are not experiencing learning or social/behavior difficulties (*primary prevention*), students who are considered to be at risk for the development of learning or social/behavior difficulties (*secondary prevention*), and students who currently are experiencing significant learning or social/behavior difficulties (*tertiary prevention*).

We can visualize this model and its three levels of prevention as a triangle. The entire triangle represents all students within a school setting, the majority of whom are not experiencing difficulties (i.e., the bottom portion of the triangle), some of whom are at risk of developing significant problems (i.e., the middle portion), and an even smaller percentage who are currently experiencing significant difficulties (i.e., the top portion). Typical practice is to focus on those students who are at the top of the triangle—those who are currently experiencing significant learning and/or social-emotional difficulties. Practitioners tend to spend the majority of their time and effort providing tertiary prevention (i.e., individualized assessment and intervention services) to these students on a case-by-case basis. These students make up the smallest percentage of the school population, but because of the significance of their problems, they often require the majority of time and resources from school personnel (Walker et al., 1996).

Shifting to a systemwide prevention model requires that we look at the "big picture" by considering the needs of all students, not just those who are referred because they are experiencing significant difficulties. The foundation of a prevention approach is the use of universal interventions (i.e., primary prevention) designed to enhance the delivery of effective instruction and improve school climate to promote academic, social, and behavioral resilience of all students in the school. This idea requires that we begin to move some resources and energy toward those children and adolescents who are not currently experiencing significant difficulties in order to help them acquire skills to reduce the probability that they will eventually rise to the "top of the triangle." More specifically, primary prevention for students who are not currently experiencing learning and/or social/behavior difficulties is accomplished through schoolwide and classwide efforts that involve the consistent use of research-based effective practices, ongoing monitoring of these practices and student outcomes, and staff training and professional development. The goal of primary prevention is to create school and classroom environments that promote student learning and health and decrease the number of students at risk for learning or social/behavior problems.

As important as it is to focus on primary prevention, we also know that not all students respond similarly to these efforts. Thus, it is important to monitor student progress and to assess whether students are at risk (i.e., in need of secondary prevention efforts) or experiencing significant difficulties (i.e., in need of tertiary prevention efforts). Identifying students at risk for learning, social-emotional, and behavior difficulties is an important aspect to comprehensive prevention efforts. For students identified as at risk and in need of secondary prevention efforts, the focus is on the delivery of specialized interventions (often at a small-group level) to prevent the worsening of problems and to prevent the development of more significant concerns. The focus on early identification and EI is important.

With respect to mental health and social-emotional problems of children and adolescents, we believe that this prevention model is an ideal way to think about providing SEL programs and other services. Thinking in this way about the challenges we face in promoting social-emotional wellness and mental health among children and adolescents makes these challenges more manageable. Instead of waiting until students have developed severe problems and require extensive time and effort to simply be managed, we can continually focus a portion of our resources on prevention activities that will ultimately reduce the number of students at the top of the triangle.

AN EVIDENCE-BASED PROGRAM

We continue to make efforts to establish a solid evidence base for *Strong Kids™: A Social and Emotional Learning Curriculum* (including *Strong Start—Grades K–2*, *Strong Kids—Grades 3–5*, *Strong Kids—Grades 6–8*, and *Strong Teens—Grades 9–12*). In 2010, Merrell reviewed the studies that had been conducted to date. Each of these studies found that groups of students who participated in one of the Strong Kids programs showed significant gains in their knowledge of curriculum concepts of SEL. Many of the studies have shown significant reductions of problem emotional-behavioral symptoms as a result of participating in the programs. In addition, some of the studies have evaluated the feasibility and acceptability of the programs from teacher and student perspectives. These studies, without exception, showed a very high amount of satisfaction and confidence in the programs by both students and teachers. They also have helped us to understand what we consider to be best practices in implementation. Since that review, a number of additional studies have been conducted with similar findings. These studies have occurred in a range of settings, primarily at the primary and secondary levels of intervention. Visit www.strongkidsresources.com to access information on these studies, or see the list below.

Strong Start, Strong Kids, and *Strong Teens*: Research

Barker, E.S., Marcotte, A.M., & Whitcomb, S.A. (2015). *Promoting positive teacher–child interactions through implementation of a social emotional learning curriculum with performance feedback.* Manuscript in revision.

Berry-Krazmien, C., & Torres-Fernandez, I. (2007, March). *Implementation of the Strong Kids curriculum in a residential facility.* Poster presentation at the Annual Convention of the National Association of School Psychologists. New York, NY.

Caldarella, P., Christensen, L., Kramer, T.J., & Kronmiller, K. (2009). Promoting social and emotional learning in second grade students: A study of the *Strong Start* curriculum. *Early Childhood Education Journal, 37,* 51–56. doi:10.1007/s10643-009-0321-4

Castro-Olivo, S. (2014). Promoting social-emotional learning in adolescent Latino ELLs: A study of the culturally adapted Strong Teens program. *School Psychology Quarterly, 29,* 567–577.

Faust, J.J. (2006). *Preventing anxiety and depression: An evaluation of social-emotional curriculum* (Unpublished educational specialist's thesis). University of Wisconsin, Whitewater.

Feuerborn, L.L. (2004). *Promoting emotional resiliency through classroom instruction: The effects of a classroom-based prevention program* (Unpublished doctoral dissertation). University of Oregon, Eugene.

Gueldner, B.A., & Merrell, K.W. (2011). The effectiveness of a social and emotional learning program with middle school students in the general education setting and the effect of consultation on student outcomes. *Journal of Educational and Psychological Consultation, 21,* 1–27. doi:10.1080/10474412.2010.522876

Gunter, L., Caldarella, P., Korth, B.B., & Young, K.R. (2012). Promoting social and emotional learning in preschool students: A study of Strong Start Pre-K. *Early Childhood Education, 40,* 151–159.

Harlacher, J.E., & Merrell, K.W. (2009). Social and emotional learning as a universal level of support: Evaluating the follow-up effect of Strong Kids on social and emotional outcomes. *Journal of Applied School Psychology, 26*(3), 212–229. doi:10.1080/15377903.2010.495903

Isava, D.M. (2006). *An investigation of the impact of a social emotional learning curriculum on problem symptoms and knowledge gains among adolescents in a residential treatment center* (Unpublished doctoral dissertation). University of Oregon, Eugene.

Kramer, T.J., Caldarella, P., Christensen, L., & Shatzer, R.H. (2010). Social and emotional learning in the kindergarten classroom: Evaluation of the *Strong Start* curriculum. *Early Childhood Education Journal, 37,* 303–309. doi:10.1007/s10643-009-0354-8

Kramer, T.J., Caldarella, P., Young, R., Fischer, L., & Warren, J.S. (2014). Implementing Strong Kids school-wide to reduce internalizing behaviors and increase prosocial behaviors. *Education and Treatment of Children, 37,* 659–680.

Levitt, V. (2009). *Promoting social-emotional competency through quality teaching practices: The impact of consultation on a multidimensional treatment integrity model of the Strong Kids program* (Unpublished doctoral dissertation). University of Oregon, Eugene.

Marchant, M., Brown, M., Caldarella, P., & Young, E. (2010). Effects of Strong Kids curriculum on students at risk for internalizing disorders: A pilot study. *Journal of Empirically Based Practices in Schools, 11*(2), 123–143.

Merrell, K.W., Juskelis, M.P., Tran, O.K., & Buchanan, R. (2008). Social and emotional learning in the classroom: Impact of Strong Kids and Strong Teens on students' social-emotional knowledge and symptoms. *Journal of Applied School Psychology, 24*, 209–224. doi: 10.1080/15377900802089981

Meyer, K.M. (2014). *Program evaluation of the Strong Start curriculum as a selected intervention for early elementary students* (Unpublished doctoral dissertation). University of Massachusetts, Amherst.

Nakayama, N.J. (2008). *An investigation of the impact of the Strong Kids curriculum on social-emotional knowledge and symptoms of elementary aged students in a self-contained special education setting* (Unpublished doctoral dissertation). University of Oregon, Eugene.

Sicotte, J.L. (2013). *Effects of Strong Start curriculum on internalizing, externalizing behaviors, and emotion knowledge among kindergarten and first grade students* (Unpublished doctoral dissertation). University of Massachusetts, Amherst.

Tran, O.K. (2008). *Promoting social and emotional learning in schools: An investigation of massed versus distributed practice schedules and social validity of the Strong Kids curriculum in late elementary aged students* (Unpublished doctoral dissertation). University of Oregon, Eugene.

Whitcomb, S.A., & Merrell, K.W. (2012). Understanding implementation and effectiveness of Strong Start K–2 on social-emotional behavior. *Early Childhood Education Journal, 40*, 63–71. doi:10.1007/s10643-011-0490-9

White, N.J., & Rayle, A.D. (2007). Strong Teens: A school-based small group experience for African American males. *The Journal for Specialists in Group Work, 32*, 178–189. doi: 10.1080/01933920701227224

REFERENCES

Collaborative for Academic, Social, and Emotional Learning. (2012). *2013 CASEL guide: Effective social and emotional learning programs—Preschool and elementary school edition.* Chicago, IL: Author.

Cowen, E.L. (1994). The enhancement of psychological wellness: Challenges and opportunities. *American Journal of Community Psychology, 22*, 149–179.

Doll, B., & Lyon, M.A. (1998). Risk and resilience: Implications for the delivery of educational and mental health services in schools. *School Psychology Review, 27*, 348–363.

Durlak, J.A., Weissberg, R.P., Dymnicki, A.B., Taylor, R.D., & Schellinger, K.B. (2011). The impact of enhancing students' social and emotional learning: A meta-analysis of school-based universal interventions. *Child Development, 82*, 405–432.

Greenberg, M.T., Domitrovich, C., & Bumbarger, B. (2001).The prevention of mental health disorders in school-age children: Current state of the field. *Prevention and Treatment, 4*(1), 1–62.

Greenberg, M.T., Weissberg, R.P., O'Brien, M.U., Zins, J.E., Fredericks, L., Resnick, H., & Elias, M. (2003). Enhancing school-based prevention and youth development through coordinated social, emotional, and academic learning. *American Psychologist, 58*, 466–474.

Merrell, K.W. (2010). Linking prevention science and social and emotional learning: The Oregon resiliency project. *Psychology in the Schools, 47*, 55–70.

Merrell, K.W., & Buchanan, R.S. (2006). Intervention selection in school-based practice: Using public health models to enhance systems capacity of schools. *School Psychology Review, 35*, 167–180.

U.S. Department of Education, OSEP Center on Positive Behavioral Interventions and Supports. (2004). *School-wide PBS.* Retrieved from http://www.pbis.org/school

Walker, H.M., Horner, R.H., Sugai, G., Bullis, M., Sprague, J.R., Bricker, D., & Kaufman, M.J. (1996). Integrated approaches to preventing antisocial behavior patterns among school-age children and youth. *Journal of Emotional and Behavioral Disorders, 4*, 194–209.

Weissberg, R.P., Walberg, H.J., O'Brien, M.U., & Kuster, C.B. (Eds.). (2003). *Long-term trends in the well-being of children and youth.* Washington, DC: Child Welfare League of America Press.

Zins, J.E., Bloodworth, M.R., Weissberg, R.P., & Walberg, H.J. (2004). The scientific base linking social and emotional learning to school success. In J. Zins, M. Wang, & H. Walberg (Eds.), *Building academic success and social-emotional learning: What does the research say?* New York, NY: Teachers College Press.

CHAPTER 2

Implementation Guidelines and Lesson Structure

Strong Start—Pre-K was developed with principles of effective instructional design and delivery in mind (Carnine, Silbert, & Kame'enui, 2009; Coyne, Kame'enui, & Carnine, 2006), and attention was given to ensure that lessons meet SAFE (i.e., sequenced, active, focused, and explicit) criteria described by Durlak and colleagues (2011). Each lesson includes instructional scaffolding (e.g., optional scripting and explicit directions) to eliminate the need for intensive preparation; a review and introduction of the lesson and key concepts; a range of examples to define the concept; and opportunities to practice and integrate skills through activities such as modeling, guided practice and role play, and independent practice. Generalization and maintenance of skills are promoted by providing strategies for practice throughout the school day, in other academic areas, and across settings.

We also prioritized implementation feasibility and social acceptability when designing this curriculum. Even an exceptionally strong intervention program will fail to make an impact if its time requirements and difficulty of implementation result in few people being able to use it within the time and training constraints of a school system or other youth-serving agency. We recommend teaching the *Strong Start—Pre-K* lessons once per week for 10 weeks, although there is evidence to support implementation at a more accelerated tempo such as two lessons per week with similar effective outcomes (Tran, 2008). The one lesson per week format may allow students sufficient time to complete any extension activities that may be assigned, internalize the concepts taught, and practice the new skills they learn, both at school and outside of school.

Each lesson takes about 25 minutes to complete. All lessons can be segmented into parts. Please refer to the Running Short on Time? section for ideas for breaking up lessons. This is a particularly important consideration given that the attention span and needs of preschoolers may be very different from those of students in elementary school. Lessons can also be lengthened with additional extension activities found at the end of each lesson.

Strong Start—Pre-K is highly structured and semiscripted, designed to cover very specific objectives and goals. We developed the objectives and goals for each lesson, as well as the implementation guidelines, based on current research findings in education and psychology, aiming for a prevention and intervention program that is built on a solid base of empirical evidence. Each lesson follows a similar format with the following sections:

- SEL Competencies: The Collaborative for Academic, Social, and Emotional Learning (CASEL, 2012) endorses five key areas necessary in building SEL skills (self-awareness, self-management, social awareness, relationship skills, and responsible decision making). Skills categories are assigned to each lesson where content reflects these areas.

- Purpose and Objectives: describes the skills students will learn

- Materials Needed: lists the materials needed for advance preparation

- Running Short on Time?: suggests an optional stopping point to segment the lesson

- Instructor Reflection: provides an opportunity for instructors to reflect on the content of the lesson to increase knowledge and personalized application

- Review: lists topics covered in the previous lesson

- Introduction: introduces the concepts for the lesson

- Optional Focusing Activity: mindfulness-based activity to help students focus and prepare for the lesson

- Read a Book from the Literature List: provides a list of suggested children's literature and guiding discussion questions that are connected to the goals and objectives of each lesson

- Instructional Content and Practice Activities: specialized to each lesson's theme

- Closure: review of content covered

- Applying What We Learned: considerations for embedding skill practice across the day

- Extension Activities: additional activities to integrate into the day

- *Strong Start* Bulletin: informational newsletter to communicate important language, skills, and strategies to families

Each lesson provides optional scripts to aid content delivery, sample situations and examples to better illustrate the content, and opportunities for guided and independent practice. We encourage group leaders to review scripts before lesson implementation so that they can think about how they can best communicate lesson content. Scripts can be used verbatim or simply as a guide. In addition, we encourage group leaders to review and perhaps modify examples and scenarios given about each of the concepts, because it might be more helpful for students to learn from actual examples and scenarios that have happened in their classroom, school, or home contexts. At the end of Lessons 2 through 10 is a section titled Applying What We Learned and another titled Extension Activity. These sections aim to reinforce concepts that were explicitly taught.

The Applying What We Learned section of *Strong Start* prompts group leaders to *anticipate* situations and occasions when students may have opportunities to practice skills learned. In anticipating these times, instructors can proactively support student practice. This section also gives ideas for how to *remind* students to use *Strong Start* skills at relevant times. Finally, we suggest that teachers *acknowledge* students for appropriate use of skills learned. This will make it more likely that students will use their skills again in the future.

Each extension activity is an optional activity that provides additional skills practice and opportunities to embed lesson content into other academic subject areas. There are other activities included here that allow students to apply concepts they have learned to art projects and interactive games.

PREPARING YOUR LESSONS AND YOUR STUDENTS

Strong Start—Pre-K is designed to be used primarily with children in preschool. This age range translates to about age 3 through age 5. Obviously, there are important differences in the skills and developmental level of children at the two ends of the intended age or grade range. For this reason, we have included suggestions within the lessons for using them with younger or lower-performing students. By limiting the need for reading by students, simplifying examples and language, and reducing some of the time or behavioral demands of different lesson components, *Strong Start—Pre-K* can be used effectively with children at the younger end of the intended grade and age range. Likewise, the curriculum can be made more relevant for typically developing and high-performing children at the higher end of the grade age range by using components that require some basic reading skills, increasing the range and complexity of examples and language, and increasing the time and participation demands. As you prepare in advance to teach a *Strong Start—Pre-K* lesson, consider the developmental level of your children, and look carefully at the suggestions for adapting the lesson for younger children, if necessary.

MATERIALS NEEDED

To implement *Strong Start—Pre-K*, you should have access to a copy machine, chart paper, and a chalk or marker board. Some teachers and group leaders have found that they prefer to make and enlarge paper copies of the supplementary pictures for display in the classroom. Some of the lessons also include reproducible templates for handouts or worksheets for students, and all of the lessons include a *Strong Start* Bulletin to be personalized, duplicated, and sent home to parents to reinforce the lesson goals. These items can also be found online (see About the Downloadable Material).

An important part of our lesson development throughout *Strong Start—Pre-K* is the use of a stuffed animal "mascot" for the curriculum. In the lessons, we have given the example of a stuffed bear by the name of Henry. You may follow our suggestion by locating a stuffed bear and naming it Henry, or you may use any type of stuffed animal and name that you think is most appropriate for your children. We have found that children especially enjoy this aspect of the curriculum. The mascot becomes not only a symbol for the program but also a reminder to practice *Strong Start* skills and a welcome part of your classroom or group environment.

Some teachers who have used *Strong Start—Pre-K* found that displaying the stuffed animal in a prominent place in the classroom served as a constant reminder of the program and the skills that were being taught and that their students often asked about the next lesson or previous activities by the prompt of this display. In addition, we recommend that you not only use the mascot when teaching *Strong Start—Pre-K* but also throughout the school year. Picking up the stuffed animal from time to time, weeks or months after completing *Strong Start—Pre-K*, can serve as a keen reminder of what was learned in the program and can help support continued practice and discussion of the critical concepts and skills that were taught.

SUPPLEMENTARY MATERIALS

Each *Strong Start—Pre-K* lesson includes one or more sheets of related or supplementary materials, which are found at the end of the lesson and are available online. These materials are labeled throughout the text with a reminder symbol. For the sake of consistency, we refer to these materials as "supplements" and have titled them that way. These supplements include reproducible handouts and the *Strong Start* Bulletins for parents and family members. As you prepare for each lesson, note the supplements for that lesson and how they should be used. Prior to teaching the lesson, make copies or prepare to project images as needed. These supplements are all reproducible for users of the curriculum. Although we have made suggestions regarding how to use the supplementary materials, you should feel free to adapt them to your own needs and situation. For example, as mentioned previously, you might find it useful to enlarge some of the handouts into posters and to place them on the wall of the classroom to reinforce or visually prompt students as they learn and practice the skills promoted in *Strong Start*.

INSTRUCTOR REFLECTION

To some extent, teaching children to become more self-aware and socially aware requires a certain level of personal awareness on the part of the group leader. At the start of each lesson, there are guiding questions for the group leader to reflect on. These questions prompt leaders to consider their own skill sets as well as observations of their students' current development.

PROVIDING AN AGENDA

It is recommended that you inform your students before the class begins what the agenda or goals will be for that day's lesson. With children who can read, a written outline of the topics included in the curriculum may be useful as well as an agenda for the individual lesson. With children who are not yet skilled readers, a brief verbal overview will suffice.

STATING EXPECTED BEHAVIORS

Because of the nature of the lessons in *Strong Start—Pre-K*, behavior expectations for students or group members must be very clear. Some of the units revolve around sensitive issues, and every opportunity should be taken to provide instruction and subsequent reinforcement for appropriate behavior. Students should feel free to share their beliefs and feelings on the targeted topics but must not feel pressured into revealing anything that makes them feel uncomfortable. You should state expected behaviors before instruction, before modeling examples, and before the practice sections of lessons. In some cases, you may need to teach and reinforce behavioral expectations more frequently than at these suggested times.

As a general recommendation for promoting appropriate behavior in school and related settings, we recommend that teachers and group leaders develop and teach a few simple rules for appropriate behavior. Rules should be stated *positively*, meaning that they should tell students what is expected rather than what to avoid. For example, *respect your classmates* is a positively stated rule, whereas *no fighting* is a negatively stated rule that does not tell students what specifically they should do. Rules should be simple and appropriate to the developmental level of the children for whom they are intended. In addition, the list of rules should be kept to a minimum. Usually, no more than five general rules are needed. You will find that rules are more effective when you teach them to students, then find frequent opportunities to reinforce the rules through reminders, examples, and so forth.

PLANNING FOR SMOOTH TRANSITIONS

Time is one of the most precious commodities in your classroom or center. In a brief curriculum such as *Strong Start—Pre-K*, the element of time is especially critical. To make the best use of your limited time in teaching the curriculum, use your transition time wisely before and during the *Strong Start—Pre-K* lessons. We recommend that you have all materials prepared and organized for easy distribution to students. Make sure that equipment is in working order before you start the lessons. *Explicitly state directions before and during transitions.* If possible, precorrect for any possible behavioral difficulties.

PHYSICAL ARRANGEMENTS

For the lessons in this curriculum, all students must have a clear view of you, the group leader. For younger children, seating them in a semicircle or horseshoe arrangement on the floor for parts of the lessons (e.g., the children's books, the demonstrations) may be appropriate. You may want to preassign students to groups of two or three because they will be required to separate into groups during the application sections in some of the lessons. This will not only save time but also will give you control of which students will be paired. Always use movement, voice level, and voice intonation to increase the interest of your students and consequently increase active participation.

ADAPTATIONS FOR UNIQUE NEEDS

In many of the *Strong Start—Pre-K* lessons, you will be encouraged to create scenarios pertaining to a certain topic. To facilitate and encourage student participation, think of scenarios that would best reflect the interests, abilities, and level of understanding of the students in your class or group. You may choose to use current situations relevant to your classroom or school or even global current events to illustrate the concepts. The scenarios provided in the units should be considered examples and can be modified extensively to best fit the unique needs of your students. Making appropriate adaptations for the unique needs of your students will not only make the delivery of lessons go more smoothly but will aid with generalization and maintenance of new skills.

SUGGESTIONS FOR SUCCESS

As you teach the *Strong Start—Pre-K* lessons, you will increase your likelihood of success by observing and following a few additional suggestions for successful implementation of the curriculum:

- Initiative Alignment: Prior to implementation, take some time to think about how you can help your students make connections between *Strong Start—Pre-K* content and other schoolwide or classwide initiatives in place. For example, if your school is one that is organized around Program-Wide Positive Behavioral Interventions and Supports (PWPBIS), in which there are programwide behavioral expectations taught across all settings (see www.pbis.org for more information), you might think about how you can help your students to understand how some of the concepts in *Strong Start—Pre-K* are connected to schoolwide expectations. Similarly, many schools have specific interventions in place to limit bullying behaviors. Consider how *Strong Start* skills might overlap with or support some of the anti-bullying strategies.

- Behavior Management: Introduce or reintroduce a *behavior management technique,* such as a token economy, to reinforce prosocial behaviors during the unit. Remind students of school and classroom rules as well as the rules associated with this curriculum.

- Group Dynamics: As a general practice, we suggest that you *do not add new students to a group once it has already started.* Particularly when the program is taught to small groups of students rather than entire classrooms, we have found that having new students join the group once it has started can be disruptive to the group process and may result in a slowing of the flow of training, as well as a reduction in the willingness of group members to participate.

- *Strong Start* Toolboxes: Our experience has indicated that toolboxes that are specifically designated for students to store their drawings, and other materials related to *Strong Start* will help them to keep their materials organized and will reduce the amount of time needed by the teacher or group leader to start the weekly lessons. We suggest that you consider having all of your students keep a special *Strong Start* toolbox for this purpose.

- Lesson Overview: Be sure to give the children an overview of the curriculum and each lesson's purpose. Explain that a different topic/unit will be taught each week (or as frequently as possible), because students may come to expect a continuation of a certain topic as opposed to a new topic each lesson.

- Content Review: Ensure that you sufficiently review the topics from prior lessons and integrate concepts when at all possible.

- Skill Maintenance and Generalization: Acknowledge any *Strong Start* skills that you might observe, both within and outside of the teaching setting. Make sure that parents, teachers, administrators, and other staff are aware of the skills you are instructing, because your students will require frequent feedback in several settings in order for the skills to be durable and generalized.

- Children's Literature: Use the recommended *children's books*, and add your own titles as appropriate. Each lesson in *Strong Start—Pre-K* includes a 10- to 15-minute period designed to be used to read your students a book that reinforces the key concepts from that lesson. We have developed a short list of books for each lesson, and we encourage you to add and use other titles that you think are appropriate. We have a recommended list of discussion questions in each lesson that can be used with any relevant book.

- Time Guidelines: Our recommended *time allowance* for each of the lessons is approximately 25 minutes. Our experience (and the time breakdowns in the lesson plans) is based on this time length. These time allowances are only guidelines. If your children are very engaged in a particular activity and you are not under time pressure to finish it on schedule, you should feel free to let the activity continue. Likewise, if your children are having a particularly difficult time with one part of a lesson and you have additional time to spare, you should feel free to either continue beyond the time recommendation or to come back to the lesson later in the day.

- Family Newsletters: Use and personalize the *Strong Start* Bulletins, which are found at the end of each lesson and online. These bulletins, which are in the form of a brief letter, are designed to inform parents and other family members regarding the objectives and activities of each lesson. If parents use the information from these bulletins to reinforce concepts from the lessons and praise their children for engaging in lesson-related skill development, increased generalization of skills across settings may result.

CREATING A *STRONG START* COMMUNITY

In addition to the numerous suggestions provided to enhance lesson implementation, we have had the opportunity to observe several master teachers and enthusiastic families over the years who have embraced SEL and have creatively built in structures that empower students to regularly use social and emotional skills they have learned. Here are some examples we have observed.

Feelings Check-In

Many teachers have a morning routine in which students are asked to "sign in" to practice writing their names. We have observed teachers who also have jars with feelings pictures and popsicle sticks with student names written on them. In addition to signing in, students are asked to place a popsicle stick in the jar that represents how they are feeling on that day. Other teachers set aside time to do a feelings check-in with students during a morning meeting. These routines help students to practice identifying their emotions and help to build an emotion vocabulary.

Visual Reminders

Many teachers use visuals to cue students to practice *Strong Start* skills. We have observed teachers who wore t-shirts with "What would Henry do?" on them. These teachers wore the t-shirts out for recess to cue students to remember how the *Strong Start—Pre-K* mascot, Henry, would have handled certain social interactions. Teachers have also created and displayed posters, with *Strong Start* supplemental pictures hanging in designated spots in the classroom, to encourage students to recognize feelings, to practice calming strategies, and to problem solve.

Family Involvement

In addition to including families through sharing *Strong Start* bulletins, we have also observed families getting involved in other creative ways. For example, some schools have held a parent night and have provided a "training" or information session on *Strong Start—Pre-K* so that families could be fully informed about the curriculum. Some families have also organized a *Strong Start—Pre-K* literature display at the local public library so that books from the literature list could be easily accessed and shared.

ADAPTATIONS FOR CULTURALLY AND LINGUISTICALLY DIVERSE LEARNERS

As our society becomes increasingly diverse, researchers and practitioners have recognized the need to address cultural issues in curriculum development and implementation. Efforts to address cultural issues have ranged from ignoring or dismissing the need for cultural adaptations to arguing the need for culture-specific research and curricula tailored for each cultural subgroup. Between these two extreme positions has emerged a set of criteria and recommendations for making cultural adaptations to existing curricula. The cultural adaptation approach retains the core assumptions and skill domains of the existing curriculum but recommends tailoring the teaching of these concepts to the specific needs of particular groups of interest. Research supports the success of making cultural adaptations to existing social and emotional curricula for specific groups (see Castro-Olivo, 2014; Muñoz, Penilla, & Urizar, 2002; Yu & Seligman, 2002).

We began the development of the *Strong Kids—Grades 3–5*, *Strong Kids—Grades 6–8*, and *Strong Teens—Grades 9–12* curricula (the predecessors to *Strong Start*) with the assumption that no single curriculum could meet the learning needs of all students. By focusing on teaching a set of key ideas related to SEL and resilience, however, we believe that the curricula can successfully meet the needs of a wide range of students when appropriate adaptations are made. Some cultural variables that may require attention in curriculum adaptation processes include language, race/ethnicity, acculturation, socioeconomic status, sexual orientation, religion, gender, disability status, and nationality.

The Big Ideas of *Strong Start*

As we have noted, a successful curriculum adaptation process requires particular innovations and modifications to meet the needs of specific individuals and groups, but at the same time, these adaptations must retain the general concepts, or big ideas, on which the curriculum is based. With this notion in mind, we list the most important features of *Strong Start—Pre-K*, with the hope that these ideas will be taken into account when making any type of adaptation to the curriculum. With the underlying goal of improving SEL and resilience in kindergarten and primary grade children, these big ideas include the following:

- To help children to understand that social and emotional health, like physical health, requires attention and it results from specific actions and situations

- To teach children to identify and understand their own feelings

- To teach children how to identify and understand other people's feelings

- To teach children appropriate ways to express a range of feelings

- To teach children to understand the link between how they think and behave and the way that they feel

- To teach children skills to appropriately monitor and modify their feelings, thoughts, and behaviors

- To help children approach their challenges in life with a realistic sense of optimism

- To help children to learn behavioral and affective techniques to relax and remain calm in the face of stress or worries

- To teach children problem-solving skills and effective communication skills (e.g., listening, using appropriate vocalization techniques)

- To help children to learn the skills needed to make friends and be a good friend

Specific Strategies for Making Cultural Adaptations

Keeping these big ideas in mind, *Strong Start—Pre-K* may be adapted to better fit the needs of diverse children. For this purpose, we propose a few guidelines for making cross-cultural adaptations. These suggestions are based on our experiences in attempting to adapt *Strong Kids—Grades 3–5*, *Strong Kids—Grades 6–8*, and *Strong Teens—Grades 9–12* with specific cultural groups. They are also based in great measure on the premises of the American Psychological Association's Guidelines for Providers of Psychological Services to Ethnic, Linguistic, and Culturally Diverse Populations (available at http://www.apa.org/pi/oema/resources/policy/provider-guidelines.aspx).

1. Get to know your students.

   • Ask children about their cultural identities, activities, and rituals.

   • Reflect on the dominant cultural variables in your classroom and how these aspects of culture affect the way your students behave and think.

   • Identify common success and failure experiences, problem situations, and challenging life circumstances confronted by your students.

2. Get to know your students' community.

   • Visit the families and, as appropriate, the homes of children in your class or group.

   • Identify a cultural liaison (a parent or community member who identifies as a member of the target cultural group) to help you learn more about your students' culture.

   • Ask the cultural liaison to assist with the cultural adaptation process.

3. Deliver the curriculum in a manner that your students can understand.

   • Modify the language of each lesson so that your students can easily understand the key ideas.

   • Use examples and scenarios that match the lives of your students (e.g., change characters' names, include extended family, include children who use wheelchairs, use problem examples that your students have experienced).

4. Encourage tolerance.

   • Teach students ways to show respect for different cultural groups.

   • Encourage and reinforce children for respecting the examples and comments made by their peers.

   • Establish and enforce a classroom or group rule that teasing and name-calling are not allowed.

5. Become aware of variations within cultures.

   • Do not assume too much about a child's culture or ethnicity.

   • Avoid making overgeneralizations about cultural groups. Not all members of a culture act the same way.

- Examine your own values, assumptions, and worldviews and how these are the same and different from those of your students.

- Continually examine the accuracy and fairness of your assumptions about the beliefs and behaviors of different cultural groups.

6. Seek feedback.

- View the adaptation process as an ongoing process.

- Consult with children, your colleagues, and community members about the relevance and accuracy of the adaptation efforts.

- Ask the children how well the curriculum is matching their needs and life experiences.

In sum, adapting *Strong Start—Pre-K* or any other SEL curriculum for use with culturally and linguistically diverse learners may be challenging, but it is essential if the curricula are to have the most meaningful impact on the learners. The suggestions we have offered in this section may be useful as a guide to making the flexible *Strong Start—Pre-K* program appropriate for children and youth from a variety of cultural backgrounds.

REFERENCES

Carnine, D.W., Silbert, J., Kame'enui, E.J. & Tarver, S.G. (2009). *Direct instruction reading* (5th ed.). New York, NY: Pearson

Castro-Olivo, S. (2010). One size does not fit all: Adapting social and emotional learning for use in our multicultural world. In K.W. Merrell, & B.A. Gueldner (Eds.), *Social and emotional learning in the classroom: Promoting mental health and academic success* (pp. 83–102). New York, NY: Guilford.

Castro-Olivo, S. (2014). Promoting social-emotional learning in adolescent Latino ELLs: A study of the culturally adapted Strong Teens program. *School Psychology Quarterly, 29*, 567–577.

Collaborative for Academic, Social, and Emotional Learning. (2012). *2013 CASEL guide: Effective social and emotional learning programs—Preschool and elementary school edition.* Chicago, IL: Author.

Durlak, J.A., Weissberg, R.P., Dymnicki, A.B., Taylor, R.D., & Schellinger, K.B. (2011). The impact of enhancing students' social and emotional learning: A meta-analysis of school-based universal interventions. *Child Development, 82*, 405–432.

Muñoz, R.F., Penilla, C., & Urizar, G. (2002, May 8). Expanding depression prevention research with children of diverse cultures. *Prevention & Treatment, 5*. Retrieved from http://www.journals.apa.org/prevention/volume5/pre0050013c.html

Tran, O.K. (2008). *Promoting social and emotional learning in schools: An investigation of massed versus distributed practice schedules and social validity of the Strong Kids curriculum in late elementary aged students* (Unpublished doctoral dissertation). University of Oregon, Eugene.

Yu, D.L., & Seligman, M.E.P. (2002, May 8). Preventing depressive symptoms in Chinese children. *Prevention & Treatment, 5*. Retrieved from http://www.journals.apa.org/prevention/volume5/pre0050009a.html

CHAPTER 3

Overview of the Lessons

Strong Start—Pre-K consists of 10 carefully sequenced lessons designed to enhance children's cognitive, affective, and social functioning within a relatively brief period of time. Each of these lessons is overviewed in this section. You should read these descriptions carefully prior to preparing your first lesson so that you will understand the lesson sequencing and the "big ideas" behind *Strong Start—Pre-K*.

LESSON 1: THE FEELINGS EXERCISE GROUP

In the first lesson, The Feelings Exercise Group, students are introduced to *Strong Start—Pre-K*, and the purpose, goals, and practices of the program are overviewed. A general overview of the big ideas of the curriculum and its individual lessons is provided so that students will understand what they can expect over the course of the instruction as well as behavioral expectations for their participation. Important terms are introduced, as is Henry—a stuffed animal that serves as the mascot for the curriculum. Henry also is used to help introduce key concepts. Students are made aware of the importance of this curriculum so that they are able to understand why appropriate behaviors such as showing good listening, keeping a calm body, and being a friend, as well as confidentiality of shared information, are integral parts of the experience.

LESSONS 2 AND 3: UNDERSTANDING YOUR FEELINGS

The second and third lessons, Understanding Your Feelings 1 and 2, are intended to improve the emotional vocabulary, awareness, and resilience skills of students. Understanding and recognizing one's emotions is an important skill for everyone during all stages of life because people experience emotions at school, home, work, and play. Being able to recognize their emotions and react in an appropriate way, even when the emotion is not a good feeling, will allow your students to create and sustain positive relationships in school and throughout their lives.

In Understanding Your Feelings 1, students learn to identify different types of basic emotions and distinguish them as resulting in "good" or "not so good" feelings. Students learn to recognize which situations might cause them to feel a certain way. The goal of this lesson is to apply the skills learned to different situations at different times and in different settings.

In Understanding Your Feelings 2, the feelings-identification skills are extended to include how one might express different feelings—both positive and negative—in an appropriate manner. Students learn that, although it is okay to have any feeling, there are appropriate and inappropriate ways of showing or expressing feelings. Given a way of expressing a feeling, students identify the way as "okay" or "not okay." Students then have the opportunity to apply their new skills in fun application exercises, making it more likely that they will be able to generalize the new skills to other situations.

LESSON 4: UNDERSTANDING OTHER PEOPLE'S FEELINGS

The fourth lesson, Understanding Other People's Feelings, is a very basic form of empathy training, or teaching young children to discern and understand the feelings that other people experience. Many, if not most, kindergarten and primary grade students have not yet adequately learned to take the perspective of other people, so this lesson is an important step in beginning to acquire this critical people skill. Students are taught to identify common physical cues or clues to help understand how another person might be feeling. Through stories and fun activities, students are given practice in this skill to help increase the chance that they will maintain it and generalize it to other settings.

LESSON 5: WHEN YOU'RE ANGRY

The fifth lesson, When You're Angry, teaches students that all people experience anger in their lives; however, many young children are not able to understand appropriately and deal effectively with their anger. Misunderstanding anger, and an inability to appropriately manage it, often manifests itself in inappropriate behaviors such as arguments and fights, excessive sadness, and frustration. This lesson teaches students to understand the physical signs or manifestations of anger in their bodies, identify common situations that might lead people to feel angry, and determine if responses to anger are done in "Ways that Help" or "Ways that Hurt." Students also learn synonyms for *anger*. Through activities and stories, a particular emphasis is placed on developing and practicing responses to anger that are Ways that Help.

LESSON 6: WHEN YOU'RE HAPPY

The sixth lesson, When You're Happy, teaches students how to understand and express the positive emotion of happiness. Although virtually all preschool and kindergarten students can identify the feeling of happiness, most have not yet learned the connection between this emotion and their thought processes and behaviors. This lesson focuses on identifying common physical or bodily sensations associated with feeling happy, actions and situations that are more likely to lead to this positive feeling, and developing synonyms for the word *happy*. In addition, students are taught a simple technique—Happy Talk—that can help them cope with adverse situations in a positive way while being less likely to succumb to negative feelings such as sadness or anger.

LESSON 7: WHEN YOU'RE WORRIED

Learning appropriate techniques to manage stress, anxiety, and common worries is an important strategy to promote emotional resilience and prevent physical and emotional problems. In Lesson 7, When You're Worried, students are taught to apply specific behavioral, affective, and cognitive skills to situations that might cause them worry and anxiety. The same techniques that were taught for other specific feelings—understanding physical sensations, developing synonyms, and listing common situations in which the feeling might occur—are applied specifically to the emotion of worry or anxiety. Students again practice using Happy Talk, and they are taught a new skill—the Stop, Count, In, Out strategy—that they can apply specifically to help cope with worries, fears, stress, and anxiety.

LESSON 8: BEING A GOOD FRIEND

The eighth lesson, Being a Good Friend, is a very basic social skills and interpersonal skills training module for young children. In this lesson, students are taught some of the most basic interpersonal communication skills and given opportunities to practice them in realistic situations. Skills such as using a nice voice, being a good listener, making appropriate eye contact, and using appropriate body language are emphasized. A particular focus is placed on skills that will help students make friends more easily and be good friends.

LESSON 9: SOLVING PEOPLE PROBLEMS

The ninth lesson, Solving People Problems, is designed to promote awareness of useful strategies for resolving conflict between and among peers. Interpersonal conflicts can begin early in life and, if they become a continual pattern, may provide a fertile breeding ground for depression, anxiety, and negative thinking. Thus, learning appropriate and effective ways to resolve these conflicts may be a strong preventive factor for deterring emotional as well as social problems. In this lesson, students define and describe situations in which conflicts with peers might commonly occur. Through a review of the previously taught skills for coping with anger and using Happy Talk, students are taught to apply these strategies to help fix peer problems. This lesson includes practice situations in which students can learn to identify common problems that may arise with peers, and they can practice thinking about how to fix these problems and feel better.

LESSON 10: FINISHING UP!

The title of the final *Strong Start—Pre-K* lesson has a double meaning. Finishing UP! implies that this lesson is the final one in the curriculum, but also it shows how we are striving to end on a positive or upbeat note, celebrating the accomplishments that have been made through involvement with *Strong Start—Pre-K*. This lesson provides the opportunity for students to review key points and terms from the lessons presented throughout the previous several weeks. The specific *Strong Start—Pre-K* skills that students were taught in previous lessons—identifying okay and not okay feelings; defining Ways that Help and Ways that Hurt; and using Happy Talk and the Stop, Count, In, Out strategy—are all reviewed one last time to ensure competence. Henry, the stuffed animal mascot, figures prominently in this lesson and will be available to students in the future as a tangible prompt regarding the things they learned and practiced in the *Strong Start—Pre-K* curriculum.

BOOSTER LESSONS

Appendices A and B include optional Booster Lessons for use with *Strong Start—Pre-K*. These Booster Lessons cover content from the first five and last four *Strong Start—Pre-K* lessons, respectively. They are designed to be taught several weeks or months following the conclusion of the 10 *Strong Start—Pre-K* lessons, in order to help reteach and reinforce the main concepts from *Strong Start—Pre-K*. Although the Booster Lessons are optional components, we highly recommend them and urge teachers and group leaders to consider using them to make the curriculum optimally effective. We suggest that Booster Lesson 1 be taught at least 1 month after the conclusion of the 10 *Strong Start—Pre-K* lessons, and we also recommend using the Booster Lessons as two separate sessions instead of combining them into one lesson. In addition to reteaching and reinforcing the critical components of *Strong Start—Pre-K*, your students will find the Booster Lessons to be fun. We have developed a game, *Strong Start* Feelings Bingo, for use specifically in the Booster Lessons to help reteach the six basic emotions that are taught in *Strong Start—Pre-K*.

APPLYING WHAT WE LEARNED

As a teacher or group leader, you want your efforts in teaching *Strong Start—Pre-K* to result in the students continuing to use their new adaptive social-emotional skills over time and in other settings. In developing *Strong Start—Pre-K*, we specifically planned and programmed the curricula for optimal application by children across settings and over time. In technical terms, this sort of application is referred to as *maintenance and generalization*. Specifically, we have included suggestions and activities within each of the 10 *Strong Start—Pre-K* lessons that are aimed at promoting the application or generalization of new skills learned across settings other than the intervention setting (e.g., home, community, other school settings) and the maintenance of these skills over time.

At the end of all but the first lesson is a section titled Applying What We Learned. This brief section includes suggested activities and methods in the following three areas, which are based on literature on effective instructional approaches for teaching social-behavioral skills authored by Sugai and colleagues (e.g., Langland, Lewis-Palmer, & Sugai, 1998; Sugai, Bullis, & Cumblad, 1997):

- Anticipate: activities designed to help the instructor/group leader anticipate errors and difficulties that students may have in learning new skills, to maximize the efficacy in teaching new skills that are sequenced instructionally to previously taught skills

- Remind: suggestions for providing verbal or visual prompts that will help remind students of steps, sequences, skills, and actions that are needed to engage effectively in new skills as they are taught

- Acknowledge: prompts to provide acknowledgment or praise as students successfully approximate and perform the new skills they are taught in *Strong Start—Pre-K*

In addition to the suggestions in the Applying What We Learned sections, each lesson has, embedded within it, tips for instructors as they develop and model examples of new skills and help the students see the need for these skills. These suggestions are aimed at making the lessons relevant to students, thus increasing the potential effectiveness of each lesson. Appropriate activities are provided for each of the 10 lessons that are further designed to reinforce learning from the direct instructional part of the lessons. Each lesson also has a *Strong Start* Bulletin included as a supplement. These bulletins are important communication links to the home setting to help generalize new skills your students learn.

FINAL COMMENTS

Good luck as you prepare to use *Strong Start—Pre-K*. We have tested this curriculum with many teachers and mental health professionals in the United States and elsewhere and have made many improvements to it based on their feedback from experience using it with a large number of children and in a large variety of settings. Our efforts to create an effective, user-friendly, and practical mental health promotion program, coupled with the real-world experience and feedback we gained during 5 years of initial research and development, have convinced us that Strong Kids has much to offer and can be a valuable tool for supporting SEL, promoting resilience, and teaching coping skills.

REFERENCES

Langland, S., Lewis-Palmer, T., & Sugai, G. (1998). Teaching respect in the classroom: An instructional approach. *Journal of Behavioral Education, 8*, 245–262.

Sugai, G., Bullis, M., & Cumblad, C. (1997). Provide ongoing skill development and support. *Journal of Emotional and Behavioral Disorders, 5*, 55–64.

CHAPTER 4

What's New

Updates to Strong Start—Pre-K and Strong Start

Although many of the changes in *Strong Start—Pre-K* are fairly minor, we do believe that the second edition is a significant improvement and represents current research and understanding of social and emotional learning in young children. The following section includes our conceptualization of how lessons are aligned with the competencies promoted by CASEL, changes to the lesson content, and new lesson components.

SOCIAL AND EMOTIONAL COMPETENCIES

CASEL is an organization that leads efforts to promote social and emotional learning in research, policy, and practice (see www.casel.org). This organization advocates for educational settings and community agencies to ensure that children are learning about five essential personal competencies including self-awareness, self-management, social awareness, relationship skills, and responsible decision making (CASEL, 2014; Zins et al., 2004). In the second edition of *Strong Start—Pre-K*, we have aimed to explicitly align lessons to these critical competencies. At the top of each lesson, the particular competencies addressed are listed. Table 4.1 depicts the alignment between lesson content and competencies.

CHANGES TO THE CONTENT

Few changes were made to lesson content in the second edition of *Strong Start—Pre-K*. Changes primarily included shortening scripts for group leaders and incorporating more opportunities for students to learn through active engagement. We opted to move what was Lesson 7, Understanding Other People's Feelings, to now be Lesson 4. Although the content of this lesson did not change, we do believe that this new sequence of lessons is logical in that children are first learning to understand their own emotions globally and then are learning to think about others.

Other changes to lesson content included minor revisions to wording. For example, in an attempt to keep language simple for children, we originally talked about feelings being "good" or "not good." In the second edition, we worked hard to keep the language simple and understandable while also trying

Table 4.1. Lessons and social and emotional competencies

Strong Start lesson	Self-awareness	Self-management	Social awareness	Relationship skills	Responsible decision making
1. The Feelings Exercise Group	•	•			
2. Understanding Your Feelings 1	•				
3. Understanding Your Feelings 2	•	•	•		
4. Understanding Other People's Feelings			•		
5. When You're Angry	•	•			
6. When You're Happy	•	•			
7. When You're Worried	•	•			
8. Being a Good Friend	•	•	•	•	
9. Solving People Problems	•	•	•	•	•
10. Finishing UP!	•	•	•	•	•

to refrain from judgmental language that suggests uncomfortable feelings are in any way "bad." We tweaked wording in the scripts and examples so that children can understand that it is okay and important to experience all feelings, but some make us feel "good" and others make us feel "not so good on the inside." In Lesson 7, we also introduce a new term, *stuck*, to describe situations when we may be perseverating and having a hard time letting go of worries

NEW LESSON COMPONENTS

Although the lessons continue to follow a standardized format, we have added several elements to all the lessons: 1) SEL competencies (described previously), 2) suggestions for when instructors are running short on time, 3) instructor reflection, 4) optional focusing activity, 5) extension activities, and 6) fidelity checklists. We believe these changes reflect what is considered best practice in SEL programming and implementation.

Running Short on Time?

In our field tests of *Strong Start—Pre-K* and in our experiences in school, we recognize that teachers often do not have a segment of time long enough to complete an entire lesson. In response to this observation, we have included this new section at the start of each lesson. This section provides suggestions for appropriate places to consider stopping the lesson—places where it would be relatively easy for teachers to pick up and finish at another time.

Instructor Reflection

To support teachers in lesson preparation, we have added an instructor reflection component. Much of the research related to mindfulness and the social and emotional health of teachers promotes reflective practice (Meiklejohn et al., 2012). We agree with this concept and consider reflective practice to be a critical feature of planning for social and emotional instruction for children. This segment provides teachers with guiding questions that will help them reflect on lesson content as they experience it individually and as they observe students experiencing it in the classroom. Taking this time to reflect may make teaching the concepts easier.

Optional Focusing Activity

Emerging research on teaching mindfulness practices and strategies to children is promising (Meiklejohn et al., 2012). Mindfulness has roots in Eastern spiritual traditions and is "the awareness that emerges through paying attention on purpose, in the present moment, and nonjudgmentally to the unfolding experience moment by moment" (Kabat-Zinn, 2003, p. 144). Initial research on secularized approaches suggests that developmentally appropriate, regular mindfulness practice can help children pay attention, feel calm, engage in fewer problem behaviors, feel less anxious, and so forth. Example practices may include paying attention to one's breathing and/or the sounds in the environment and identifying feelings and where in the body those feelings are experienced.

Although *Strong Start—Pre-K* is not a mindfulness curriculum, we do believe that it is a related concept and that engaging in brief mindful moments may help children to pause during the course of a busy day and turn their focus to the upcoming *Strong Start* lesson. We consider skills in mindfulness to be facilitative, opening students to new learning. For this reason, at the start of each lesson, we have provided an optional focusing activity in which teachers may guide students. We chose to focus primarily on helping students direct their attention to how they are sitting and to their breathing. We suggest that students sit up tall, that they close their eyes, and that they feel their belly as they imagine that inhaling deeply is like inflating a large balloon.

Some instructors may wish to have more background information and additional training in mindfulness-based practices to better understand and implement these ideas. For additional information on mindfulness, visit our companion web site, www.strongkidsresources.com, and the following Internet sites:

- Association for Mindfulness in Education (AME)

  A collaborative association of organizations and individuals working together to provide support for mindfulness training as a component of K–12 education; http://www.mindfuleducation.org/

- Garrison Institute's Initiative on Contemplation and Education

  Working to develop the field of contemplative education for K–12 educators and classrooms; https://www.garrisoninstitute.org

- Mindfulness-Based Stress Reduction (MBSR) and the Center for Mindfulness at University of Massachusetts Medical School; http://www.umassmed.edu/cfm

Extension Activities

We are excited about this additional section because it gives teachers more ideas for reinforcing skill acquisition and practice. At the end of each lesson, this section provides journal prompts for students in kindergarten through second grade and additional creative activities for all ages. The journal prompts often give students a scenario in which Henry, the *Strong Start* mascot, is dealing with certain feelings, friends, and so forth. Students are given questions to prompt a reflective journal entry. Entries can be written or drawn, depending on the development of the students. The activities provided are different for each lesson and include art projects, interactive games, suggested videos, and so forth. We envision teachers incorporating such activities into center time or large- or small-group time.

Fidelity Checklists

Researchers have begun to take interest in the science of intervention implementation. This science is in its infancy but is critical in building an understanding of which components of programs are most essential, how often lessons should be taught and for how long, and what quality indicators ensure successful student outcomes (Sanetti & Kratochwill, 2009). Practitioners may also like to self-monitor the extent to which lessons are being implemented as designed within the curriculum. To address this point, we have included fidelity checklists with each lesson. These checklists include what we consider to be the critical components of each lesson. We suggest that teachers use these checklists to track lesson implementation, to identify parts that may have been missed, to address missing parts at a later time, and so forth.

SUMMARY

Through ongoing research and feedback gained from users, we have worked hard to create a program that is carefully designed, fun and efficient to implement, and effective in providing students with skills and strategies that will bolster their mental health at an early age. We hope that the edits and additions that we have made to this second edition are helpful to the students receiving the curriculum and to the adults delivering it.

REFERENCES

Collaborative for Academic, Social, and Emotional Learning. (2014). *Social and emotional learning core competencies.* Retrieved from http://www.casel.org/social-and-emotional-learning/core-competencies.

Kabat-Zinn, J. (2003). Mindfulness-based interventions in context: Past, present, and future. *Clinical Psychology: Science and Practice, 10*(2), 144–156.

Meiklejohn, J., Phillips, C., Freedman, M.L., Griffin, M.L., Biegel, G., Roach, A., . . . & Saltzman, A. (2012). Integrating mindfulness training into K–12 education: Fostering the resilience of teachers and students. *Mindfulness, 3*(4), 291–307. doi: 10.1007/s12671-012-0094-5

Sanetti, L., & Kratochwill, T. (2009). Toward developing a science of treatment integrity: Introduction to the special series. *School Psychology Review, 38*, 445–459. Retrieved from http://www.nasponline.org/publications/spr/sprmain.aspx

Zins, J.E., Bloodworth, M.R., Weissberg, R.P., & Walberg, H.J. (2004). The scientific base linking social and emotional learning to school success. In J. Zins, M. Wang, & H. Walberg (Eds.), *Building academic success and social-emotional learning: What does the research say?* New York, NY: Teachers College Press.

SECTION II

The *Strong Start—* Pre-K Curriculum

LESSON 1

The Feelings Exercise Group

SEL Competencies Addressed in This Lesson

Responsible decision making

Self-awareness

Relationship skills

Self-management

Social awareness

Teacher Notes

Purpose and Objectives

The purpose of this lesson is to introduce students to the *Strong Start—Pre-K* curriculum.

- Students will learn expected behaviors for participation in the program.
- Students will demonstrate a developmentally appropriate understanding of the concept of confidentiality.

Materials Needed

☐ Henry (stuffed animal mascot)

☐ Supplement 1.1 (laminated card)

☐ Book from the literature list (or one of your choice)

☐ *Strong Start* Bulletin

Running Short on Time?

This initial lesson is fairly short, but if you are still feeling short on time, you can consider segmenting this lesson into parts. You might describe the curriculum and introduce Henry on one day, and you might read and discuss a book from the literature list on another day.

Instructor Reflection

As you prepare to begin this curriculum, which focuses on helping students to build emotional awareness, coping skills, and empathy, think broadly about your own skill set. How did you learn about your own feelings when you were growing up? How aware are you of your own feelings and coping strategies? What about your students? Do they have some awareness of their feelings? What are the ways in which you have observed helpful or unhelpful coping strategies in your students? How aware are students of others' feelings? How do you typically intervene when students engage in unhelpful coping strategies?

Introduction

 3 MINS.

Communicate the lesson's purpose and objectives clearly. Explain to your students that they will be starting a new curriculum, *Strong Start*. Tell them how often it will be taught, and give examples of some of the topics that will be covered. Make it clear that the skills learned during this unit are skills that are important to their social and emotional health during all phases of life.

Throughout the lessons, we use a small stuffed bear named Henry as a class mascot. You may select a different stuffed animal or name if you wish. Introduce the children to Henry.

Sample Script

Today, we are going to begin a special class called Strong Start. In this class, we will be learning with a new friend. His name is Henry! In this class, Henry will help us understand our feelings and other people's feelings. He will also help us learn about being a good friend. We will be with Henry [once per week] for [one class period]. Every time we meet, we will do special exercises, except we won't be running around outside or lifting big, heavy weights. We will be working on growing strong on the inside, so we will call our group the Feelings Exercise Group. Everyone needs to be healthy—on the outside and on the inside. This class will help you to be healthy on the inside for your whole life.

Defining Behavior Expectations

 5 MINS.

Explain to your students that they are now part of a special group with some special rules. It is helpful to present the rules one at a time and have your students help you to determine and demonstrate examples and nonexamples of each rule. The three rules for the group are as follows:

1. Be a good listener.

2. Keep a calm body.

3. Be a friend.

Sample Script

You are now part of a special group with some special rules. The first rule is "Be a good listener." What does a good listener do? [Expect answers like eyes on the person who is talking and lips zipped.] *The next rule is "Keep a calm body." What does a calm body look like?* [Expect answers like hands to ourselves and sitting on our bottoms.] *Why do you think it is important to have a calm body when we are in the Feelings Exercise Group? The last rule is "Be a friend." What does it mean to be a friend? How can you be a friend?* [Expect answers like someone who listens to you and someone who is nice to you.]

Optional Focusing Activity Introduction

 5 MINS. Take this time to introduce the concept of mindfulness and focusing our attention. This can be fairly abstract, but there are numerous ways to accomplish this introduction more concretely, including mindful listening, breathing, and so forth. In this curriculum, we have given examples of mindful breathing. Students may feel silly at first, but after practicing routinely, the silliness will likely diminish. Core ideas to communicate with students are as follows:

- School days are busy. We are always moving, thinking, and working. Focusing activities allow us to stop briefly to calm our bodies and pay attention to how we are experiencing the current moment.

- Focusing activities can help us move from feeling all stirred up like a shaken snow globe to more calm like when the snow globe is still and the snow settles.

- To practice this activity, you must sit up straight, pretending a string is attached to the top of your head, pulling you up; sit crisscross applesauce or (if seated) with your feet on the floor, and close your eyes.

- Pretend a balloon is in your belly and when you breathe in through your nose, the balloon gets bigger. When you breathe out, the balloon deflates. Try three belly breaths.

Sample Script

Before we read our story today, let's practice focusing our energy and calming our bodies with Henry. Henry knows our days at school are very busy. We are always moving, thinking, and working. This activity will help us to stop for a minute to calm our bodies and focus on our feelings right now. When we are so busy, we might feel like a snow globe with snow floating all around. Watch Henry [shake him around]. *He has so much energy! This activity will help us to feel more calm like when the snow globe is still and all of the snow is on the ground. Watch Henry first. He sits up straight and crisscross applesauce or* [if seated] *with both feet on the ground. Let's act just like Henry. Close your eyes. Pretend there is a balloon in your belly. When you take a breath in through your nose, the balloon in your belly gets bigger. When you breathe out, the balloon gets smaller. Take three of these big breaths. Notice how you are feeling today. Try to calm your body and get ready to listen to our story. Look! Henry is calm and ready to listen, too!*

Read a Book from the Literature List

🕒 10 MINS. Read a book from the following list of examples or choose your own book to share with students.

- *Feelings* by Aliki
- *The Way I Feel* by Janan Cain
- *Feelings* by Joanne Brisson Murphy
- *The Feelings Book* by Todd Parr
- *My Many Colored Days* by Dr. Seuss

Be sure to point out all of the actions or ways in which the characters behave when they are acting on their feelings. Use the following questions to guide your discussion:

- What was one of the feelings the character had?
- Do you think it was a good or not so good feeling?
- What did the character do when he or she was feeling that way?

Introduction to the Topics Covered in the Curriculum

🕒 5 MINS. Introduce the topics, and provide a brief explanation for each of the lessons using Supplement 1.1 as a laminated card.

Sample Script

When we meet for Strong Start lessons, we will be learning lots of new things. We will learn about feeling angry, feeling happy, and feeling worried or scared. We will learn about other people's feelings, and we will learn about being a friend. We will also learn about solving problems. Finally, we will learn how to relax and feel calm.

Discuss the Concept of Confidentiality

🕒 2 MINS. Help your students understand the following ideas:

- They may be asked to share personal information during lessons.
- They have the right to pass on sharing personal stories.
- They may speak to you individually if they feel uncomfortable sharing in a large group.

Have students demonstrate that they understand these concepts.

Sample Script

During this special class, you might be asked to share stories about times when you have been very happy, mad, or sad or have had other very strong feelings such as being scared. If you want to share a story, you can raise your hand to let me know. If you start to feel like you don't want to share a story anymore, you can stop at any time. If you don't want to tell everyone your story, but you would still like to share it with me, you can talk to me after class.

When someone else is sharing a story, we will follow our special group rules—we will be good listeners, we will keep calm bodies, and we will be good friends.

Closure

 1 MIN.   Gather your students together, and review the lesson's objectives.

Sample Script

Today, we talked about our new special class called Strong Start and the Feelings Exercise Group. We also talked about the rules of our group, which are 1) be a good listener, 2) keep a calm body, and 3) be a friend. This class will help us learn how to be healthy on the inside for the rest of our lives, and Henry is going to help us. I am excited to start this special class with you!

About *Strong Start*

We will learn about our feelings.

feeling *angry*   feeling *happy*   feeling *worried*

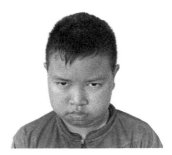      

We will learn about other people's feelings.

We will learn about being a friend.

We will learn how to relax and feel calm.

And we will learn about solving problems.

Merrell's Strong Start—Pre-K: A Social and Emotional Learning Curriculum, Second Edition, by Sara A. Whitcomb and Danielle M. Parisi Damico.

 **Strong Start Bulletin**

Dear Family,

Today, your child participated in the first lesson of **Strong Start—Pre-K**, a curriculum designed to boost the social and emotional development of young children. This curriculum includes 10 lessons that help children in recognizing and managing emotions, engaging in problem solving, and being a good friend. Your child was introduced to **Henry**, a stuffed bear who will serve as an important figure in the classroom community and in all lessons included in this curriculum. Today's lesson, titled **The Feelings Exercise Group**, focused on helping children realize that it is just as important to be emotionally strong as it is to be physically strong. Below are examples of the vocabulary and pictures presented during today's lesson.

Strong Start Objectives

To learn about our feelings

To learn about other people's feelings

To learn about being a friend

To learn about solving problems

And to learn how to relax and feel calm

Over the next several weeks, you will be receiving bulletins that detail the content of all of the **Strong Start** lessons. To help your child use the skills he or she learns, be sure to read the letters and try out the suggested strategies at home.

Thank you in advance for supporting your child as he or she learns about the important topics covered in **Strong Start**. If you notice your child using skills he or she has learned at school, be sure to applaud your child's efforts!

Fidelity Checklist

I. Introduction

- ☐ Explain to students that a new curriculum will be started.
- ☐ Give examples of what will be taught and the importance of social and emotional health.
- ☐ Introduce "Henry."

II. Defining Behavior Expectations

- ☐ List rules for the group.
- ☐ Discuss the importance of each expectation.

III. Discussion of Confidentiality

- ☐ Explain that students can choose to share personal stories or not.
- ☐ Instruct students to tell stories without naming names.

IV. Introduction to the Topics Covered

- ☐ Use Supplement 1.1 to introduce topics.
- ☐ Review topics orally.

V. Read a Book from the Literature List

Book Title/Author: _____

- ☐ Help students to identify characters' feelings and behaviors.
- ☐ Use relevant questions to guide the discussion.

VI. Closure

- ☐ Review with students that they will be learning about life skills.
- ☐ Remind students about class rules.

LESSON 2

Understanding Your Feelings 1

SEL Competencies Addressed in This Lesson

Teacher Notes

_____

_____

_____

_____

_____

_____

_____

_____

Purpose and Objectives

The purpose of this lesson is to teach students to recognize and name basic feelings.

• Students will name feelings that make them feel good or not so good on the inside.

Materials Needed

☐ Henry (stuffed animal mascot)

☐ Chart paper

☐ Supplements 2.1–2.6 (laminated cards)

☐ Supplement 2.7 (PDF document)

☐ Paper plates

☐ Cut-out feelings pictures (six feelings per student)

☐ Construction paper arrows (one per student)

☐ Brad fasteners (one per student)

☐ Book from the literature list (or one of your choice)

☐ _Strong Start_ Bulletin

Running Short on Time?

Consider segmenting the lesson. You may choose to introduce the lesson and read a book from the literature list with guiding discussion questions during one mini-lesson. You may then follow up with generating a list of feelings and identifying good and not so good feelings at another time. Additional activities can happen at any time prior to introduction of the next lesson.

Instructor Reflection

To best prepare for this lesson, think about how you identify your own feelings and the feelings of your students. Do you have particular physical cues that help you identify certain feelings (e.g., sweaty palms, butterflies in your stomach)? How do you know when you feel good versus not so good on the inside? Think of specific examples of each to model for students. How do you know when your students feel good versus not so good on the inside? What are some of the situations in your classroom when you notice a range of emotions (e.g., new activities, changes in routines)?

Review

 1 MIN.   To activate prior knowledge, review and discuss previous topics and main ideas. Obtain one to two adequate ideas. Make sure to provide feedback.

Sample Script

During our last meeting, we introduced you to Henry and we talked about exercising our feelings, just like we exercise other muscles in our bodies when we want to make them stronger. Raise your hand if you can tell me one reason that it is important to exercise your feelings. What is an important idea we learned during that lesson?

Introduction

1 MIN.   Communicate clearly the lesson's purpose and objectives.

Sample Script

Today, Henry has come back to help us learn how to name our feelings. We will talk about all different kinds of feelings and how they make us feel good or not so good on the inside.

Optional Focusing Activity

Sample Script

Before we start our lesson today, let's practice calming our bodies. Sit crisscross applesauce. Close your eyes. Pretend you have a balloon in your belly and take a deep breath in through your nose, blowing up that balloon. Breathe out through your mouth, making the balloon small. Take three more balloon breaths. Now let's get ready to use careful listening for our story.

Read a Book from the Literature List

⏱ 10 MINS. Read a book from the following list of examples or choose your own book to share with students.

- *Everybody Has Feelings/Todos Tenemos Sentimientos: The Moods of Children* by Charles E. Avery

- *My First Day at Nursery School* by Becky Edwards

- *How Are You Peeling? Foods with Moods* by Saxton Freymann and Joost Elffers

- *On Monday When It Rained* by Cherryl Kachenmeister

- *My Many Colored Days* by Dr. Seuss

Be sure to point out all of the actions or ways in which the characters behave when they are acting on their feelings. Use the following questions to guide your discussion:

- What was one of the feelings the character had?

- Do you think it was a good or a not so good feeling?

- What did the character do when he or she was feeling that way?

- Can you think of a time when you felt that way? What kind of face can you make to show that feeling?

Feelings Identification

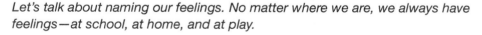

⏱ 10 MINS. Explain to students that you will be discussing feelings and labeling them as those that make us feel good or not so good on the inside.

Sample Script

Let's talk about naming our feelings. No matter where we are, we always have feelings—at school, at home, and at play.

Use Supplements 2.1–2.6 to guide your discussion about feelings.

1. Generate a list of feelings.

- State a basic emotion, such as happy or sad, and explain that this is a feeling. Show the picture that goes with that feeling and help children understand the facial features that help to tell what feeling it is (e.g., a happy face shows a smile). Ask for one or two volunteers to demonstrate the facial features associated with that feeling.

- Give a second example, using a more complex emotion such as angry or surprised. Show the picture that goes with each feeling. Ask for one or two volunteers to demonstrate the facial features associated with that feeling.

- Repeat this process until you have shown all six feelings pictures.

2. Identify feelings that may make us feel good or not so good.

- Model this skill using all of the feelings you and the students named in Step 1.

Sample Script

Good feelings and not so good feelings feel very different inside your body. Happy is a good feeling. When I feel happy, I feel good, and I like to smile. Sad is a not so good feeling. When I feel sad, I feel bad and unhappy, and I may even cry.

- Go back to the start of your list, and have the students stand up for feelings that make people feel good on the inside and sit down for feelings that make people feel not so good on the inside.

Sample Script

Another way you could show that feelings are good or not so good is to stand up or sit down. When I show a picture and say the feeling that goes with it, I want you to stand up if it makes you feel good and sit down if it makes you feel not so good. Remember, not all of you will feel the same way about all feelings. For example, when I feel surprised, I feel good, but Henry does not like surprised feelings. They make him feel not so good on the inside.

"If You're Happy and You Know It"

 2 MINS. Encourage students to stand up and follow your lead in singing "If You're Happy and You Know It." Use the following script as a guide, and add any additional feelings as you see fit. Display Supplements 2.1–2.6 if desired.

Sample Script

If you're happy and you know it, clap your hands.
If you're sad and you know it, say, "Boo hoo."
If you're afraid and you know it, take a breath.
If you're angry and you know it, use your words.
If you're surprised and you know it, say, "Wowee!"
If you're disgusted and you know it, say, "Yucky."

Closure

 1 MIN. Gather your students together and review the lesson objectives.

Sample Script

Today, we learned how to name our feelings. We learned how to name different kinds of feelings. We talked about how feelings make us feel good or not so good on the inside, and we talked about times when we have different feelings.

Everyone has feelings at school, at home, and at play. Being able to name our feelings is important because if we know how to name our feelings and can talk about them, it will help us to know what to do even if the feeling makes us feel not good on the inside.

Activity: How Do You Feel?

 15 MINS. *Complete this activity before implementation of the next lesson.*

- Use this time to brainstorm examples of how people might feel at different times. Model examples of times when you felt happy or sad.

Sample Script

We all have feelings every day. Some days, we might feel happy, and on other days, we might have different feelings. For example, today, Henry is feeling happy because he is here with all of you. Yesterday, he felt afraid because he watched a scary movie.

- Encourage children to participate in making a feelings wheel so that they can point an arrow to how they feel. Give each child a paper plate that has been divided into six pie pieces with a marker. Give children cut-out pictures of each of the six basic feelings. Have children glue one feeling to each section of their plates, and then help children fasten a construction paper arrow to the center of their plates.

- At the conclusion, show children how they can use their feelings wheels to share how they are feeling on that day. If appropriate and students are willing, invite two or three students to share how they are feeling.

Applying What We Learned

Anticipate

Tell your students to try to name the feelings they experience throughout the day. Once they identify or label the feelings they are experiencing, encourage them to investigate whether the feelings make them feel good or not so good on the inside. This exercise might be particularly helpful on days that will likely include more intense emotions (e.g., field trips).

Remind

If you notice students having difficulty expressing themselves in words (e.g., getting frustrated and showing it by rolling their eyes, feeling tired or upset and expressing it by putting their heads on the table), remind them to tell you what they are feeling using the words, feelings labels, or feelings wheels that were part of the lesson. Initially, it may be helpful to model use of such vocabulary (e.g., "It looks like you are feeling happy today. I can see that you have a big smile. Do you feel good on the inside?").

Acknowledge

Praise your students (or give them a small reward if you have a behavior management system in your classroom) if you notice them expressing a feeling or expressing that their feelings make them feel good or not so good on the inside (e.g., "Sally called me a name, and it made me feel not so good on the inside," or "My mom bought me a new toy, and it made me feel good on the inside").

Extension Activity: How Are You Feeling?

Purpose and Objectives

The purpose of this extension activity and/or morning meeting chart is for students to recognize and name their basic feelings, as well as to name feelings that make them feel good or not so good on the inside. Consider creating a chart for this one day, or think of ways you could create a laminated chart for students to identify feelings as a daily practice.

Materials

- ☐ Chart paper
- ☐ Marker
- ☐ Glue, tape, and scissors

- ☐ Supplement 2.7

Materials to prepare ahead of time:

- Create chart with columns for emotions faces to be pasted.
- Make enough copies and cut out faces on Supplement 2.7 for class.

Procedure

1. Have students identify how they are feeling, choose a face, and paste it in the matching column on the chart.

2. When the teacher reviews the chart, have students give a thumbs up if the emotion is a good feeling or a thumbs down if the emotion is a not so good feeling.

Basic Feelings

Happy

Basic Feelings

Sad

Basic Feelings

Afraid

Basic Feelings

Angry

Basic Feelings

Surprised

Basic Feelings

Disgusted

Basic Feelings

Basic Feelings

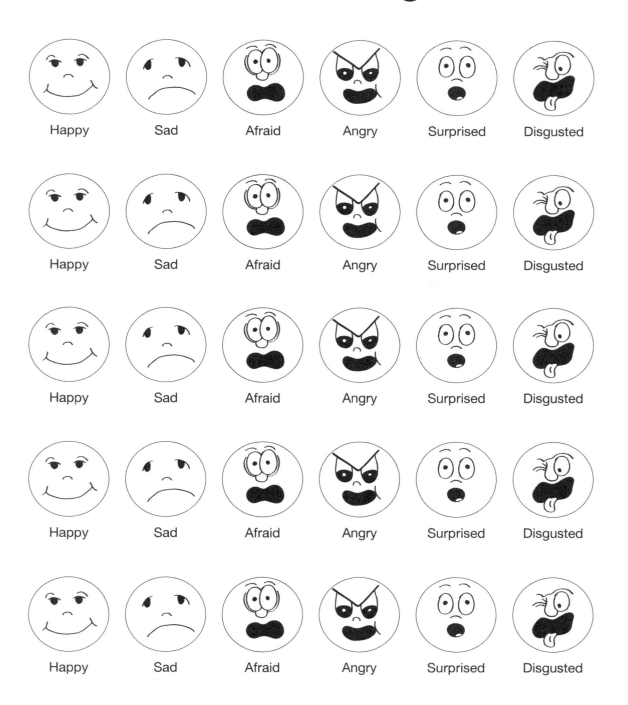

| Happy | Sad | Afraid | Angry | Surprised | Disgusted |

 **Strong Start Bulletin**

Dear Family,

This week, our **Strong Start** lesson focused on identifying and understanding the **six basic feelings** reflected below. We reviewed the names of feelings and discussed that some make us feel **good** on the inside while others make us feel **not so good.** We talked about how we might have different feelings on different days, and we also made a feelings wheel to show how we are feeling. Throughout the lesson, Henry helped us understand that it is natural for everyone to experience all feelings.

Basic Emotions

| Happy | Sad | Afraid | Angry | Surprised | Disgusted |

To better understand feelings, you could sing this song:

If you're happy and you know it, clap your hands.
If you're sad and you know it, say, "Boo hoo."
If you're afraid and you know it, take a breath.
If you're angry and you know it, use your words.
If you're surprised and you know it, say, "Wowee!"
If you're disgusted and you know it, say, "Yucky."

★ At Home

At home encourage your child to do the following:

• Stop and name the feeling he or she is experiencing.
• Determine whether the feeling is a good or not so good feeling.

The following are great examples of relevant stories that you may want to read at home:

On Monday When It Rained by Cheryl Kachenmeister

My First Day at Nursery School by Becky Edwards

Everybody Has Feelings / Todos Tenemos Sentimientos by Charles E. Avery

Thanks for supporting your child as he or she learns about identifying feelings. If you notice your child naming his or her feelings or expressing feelings that make him or her feel good or not so good on the inside, be sure to acknowledge your child's efforts!

Fidelity Checklist

I. Review

☐ Refer to the previous lesson describing the Feelings Exercise Group.

☐ Question students regarding what has been learned.

II. Introduction

☐ Communicate that students will talk about naming feelings.

☐ Communicate that there are feelings that make us feel **good** or **not so good** on the inside.

III. Feelings Identification

☐ Communicate that we all have feelings wherever we go.

☐ Generate a list of feelings.

☐ Use the pictures to show the facial features that accompany feelings.

☐ Identify feelings as those that make us feel **good** and **not so good** on the inside.

☐ Engage children in a practice activity (stand up up/sit down).

☐ Communicate that not all students will feel the same way about different feelings.

☐ Lead students in singing "If You're Happy and You Know It."

IV. Read a Book from the Literature List

Book Title/Author:_____

☐ Help students to identify characters' feelings and behaviors.

☐ Use relevant questions to guide the discussion.

V. Closure

☐ Review with students that naming feelings is important.

☐ Remind students that we have feelings everywhere we go.

☐ Review that some feelings make us feel **good** and others make us feel **not so good** on the inside.

LESSON 3

Understanding Your Feelings 2

SEL Competencies Addressed in This Lesson

Responsible decision making

Self-awareness

Relationship skills

Self-management

Social awareness

Teacher Notes

_____

_____

_____

_____

_____

_____

_____

_____

Purpose and Objectives

The purpose of this lesson is to teach students appropriate ways of expressing feelings.

- Students will continue to practice identifying basic feelings.

- Students will learn okay and not okay ways of showing feelings.

Materials Needed

☐ Henry (stuffed animal mascot)

☐ Chart paper

☐ Supplements 3.1–3.6 (laminated cards)

☐ Supplement 3.7 (PDF document)

☐ Book from the literature list (or one of your choice)

☐ *Strong Start* Bulletin

Running Short on Time?

Consider segmenting the lesson. You may choose to introduce the lesson and read a book from the literature list with guiding questions. You may follow up with another lesson period that includes discussion of having mixed-up feelings, having different feelings than others during the same situation, and handling emotions. Additional activities can be completed at any time prior to the introduction of the next lesson.

61

Instructor Reflection

To best prepare for this lesson, think about examples of times when you have perhaps felt more than one feeling at the same time. How do you know when you are mixed up? Do you have certain physical cues? How do you handle not so good feelings in ways that help? What are some of the confusing feelings that children might experience in your classroom? Can you think of situational examples? What are okay responses to not so good feelings?

Review

 2 MINS. To activate prior knowledge, review and discuss previous topics and main ideas. Prompt students to remember the six basic feelings: happy, sad, angry, afraid, surprised, and disgusted. Make sure to provide feedback.

Sample Script

During our last meeting, we learned to name our feelings. Raise your hand if you can remember a feeling that we learned about in our last class.

Introduction

 1 MIN. Communicate the lesson's purpose and objectives clearly.

Sample Script

Today, we are going to learn more about feelings. I have brought Henry to help us as we do this.

Optional Focusing Activity

Sample Script

Before we start our lesson today, let's practice calming our bodies. Sit crisscross applesauce. Close your eyes. Remember our big balloon breaths? Pretend you have a balloon in your belly and take a deep breath in through your nose, blowing up that balloon. Breathe out through your mouth, making the balloon small. Take three more balloon breaths. Now let's get ready to use careful listening for our story.

Read a Book from the Literature List

 10 MINS. Read a book from the following list of examples or choose your own book to share with students.

- *The Chocolate-Covered-Cookie Tantrum* by Deborah Blumenthal
- *The Way I Feel* by Janan Cain

- *The Feelings Book* by Todd Parr
- *Lots of Feelings* by Shelley Rotner
- *Sometimes I Like to Cry* by Elizabeth Stanton and Henry B. Stanton

Be sure to point out all of the actions or ways in which the characters behave when they are acting on their feelings. Use the following questions to guide your discussion:

- What was one of the feelings the character had/the book talked about?
- Do you think it was a good or not so good feeling?
- What did the character do when he or she was feeling that way?
- Was it an okay or not okay way of showing the feeling?
- Can you think of a time that you had that feeling?

Understanding Basic Emotions

 5 MINS. Present pictures of each of the six basic feelings using Supplements 3.1–3.6. Have students stand up and show with their faces what each of the feelings looks like.

Sample Script

This is a picture of disgust. Disgust is not a good feeling. Raise your hand if you can show me a disgusted face.

Ways of Showing Feelings

 3 MINS. Convey the following main ideas to your students:

- Everyone has feelings, and it is okay to have any feeling.
- We have different feelings at different times.
- It is important to talk about what we are feeling on the inside.
- There are okay and not okay ways to show feelings.

Sample Script

Everyone has feelings, and it is okay to have any feeling. We have different feelings at different times. When Henry is playing outside, he feels happy, and when it is cold and rainy and he has to stay inside, he feels sad. There are different ways to show our feelings. When Henry eats broccoli, he has a feeling of disgust, which is a yucky feeling. He chews it up and spits it out on the table. This is not an okay way of showing disgust because Henry wasn't showing good manners. Instead, when Henry's mom makes broccoli for dinner, Henry can say, "No, thank you." This is an okay way of showing disgust because Henry is showing good manners.

Okay and Not Okay
Examples of Showing Other Feelings

 5 MINS. The following additional examples may reflect similar situations that the children share. Use them to guide your thinking as you plan for this lesson. It might be helpful to use Henry as a puppet and have him act out okay and not okay ways to show feelings.

Have students stand up if the example suggests an okay way of showing feelings and stay seated if the example is not an okay way of showing feelings.

Feeling	Example	Okay	Not okay
Sad	Henry's dog runs away.	Henry tells you how he is feeling.	Henry screams and demands a new pet.
Angry	A friend borrowed Henry's toy car without asking.	Henry takes a deep breath and uses nice words to tell his friend how he is feeling.	Henry pulls the car out of his friend's hand.
Surprised	Henry sees his preschool teacher at the grocery store.	Henry gives his teacher a little wave.	Henry hides behind the counter and hopes she will not see him.
Afraid	Henry has to go to the doctor.	Henry tells his parents how he is feeling.	Henry keeps his feelings a secret and gets a tummy ache.

Closure

 1 MIN. Gather your students together and review the lesson objectives.

Sample Script

We all have feelings. Today, we learned that there are okay and not okay ways of showing feelings. It is all right to have any feeling, but it is important that we show our feelings in okay ways.

Applying What We Learned

Anticipate

Tell your students to remember to practice naming their feelings and using okay ways to show their feelings. It might be helpful to prompt them prior to potentially emotional times of the day, such as at recess, during choice time, or when making the transition between activities.

Remind

Similar to the last lesson, if you notice students having difficulty expressing their feelings (e.g., saying, "He is not sharing. I hate him!"), remind them that these are not okay ways to express their feelings, and ask them to try it again in an okay way. Initially, you might have to model an okay way of expressing the particular feeling (e.g., "Watch me and listen. When you don't share, it makes me feel angry").

Acknowledge

Praise your students for displaying okay ways of expressing their feelings. Some examples of okay ways could include students using "I feel" statements, talking (not yelling) about their issues with one another, or asking for help if they are getting frustrated.

Extension Activity: Additional Practice Showing Feelings

Purpose and Objectives

The purpose of this extension activity is to provide additional practice with identifying feelings by reviewing the six basic feelings and distinguishing between okay and not okay ways of expressing feelings. This could be an appropriate small-group activity.

Materials

- ☐ Supplement 3.7
- ☐ Magazines
- ☐ Glue sticks

Materials to prepare ahead of time:

- Cut out images of eyes, noses, and mouths or even ears. Make sure to include a balanced proportion of races, especially reflective of students typically less represented in media. Glasses around the eyes or earrings on the ears can highlight individual characteristics.

Procedure

Give students the feelings bubbles in Supplement 3.7. Read the bubble aloud and have students use the pictures to create the appropriate feeling and paste it on the paper.

Basic Feelings

Happy

Basic Feelings

Sad

Basic Feelings

Afraid

Basic Feelings

Angry

Basic Feelings

Surprised

Basic Feelings

Disgusted

Feelings Bubbles

_____ (student) is feeling
_____ (emotion)

because _____
(event). _____ (student) reacts
by _____
(action).

Is this okay or not okay? (circle one)

_____ (student) is feeling:

(put picture to the right)

_____ (student) is feeling
_____ (emotion)

because _____
(event). _____ (student)
reacts by
_____ (action).

Is this an okay or not okay way to show a feeling? (circle one)

_____ (student) is feeling:

(put picture to the right)

(continued)

Henry is feeling sad because his dog ran away.

Henry tells you how he is feeling.

Is this as okay or not okay way to show his feeling?

Henry is feeling:

(put picture to the right)

Carmen is feeling angry. She is tired because her sister was up crying all night.

Carmen yells "NO" when it is time to wake up after naptime.

Is this an okay or not okay way to show her feelings?

Carmen is feeling:

(put picture to the right)

(continued)

Jaleek is feeling happy because he played with his friend on the slide.

Jaleek smiled and waited in line with his friend to go again.

Is this an okay or not okay way to show his feelings?

Jaleek is feeling:

(put picture to the right)

Aida is disgusted because it is spaghetti and meatballs for lunch in the cafeteria.

Aida yells and then hits her friend.

Is this an okay or not okay way to show her feelings?

Aida is feeling:

(put picture to the right)

(continued)

Tay'von is feeling surprised because he blocked the goal.

Tay'von smiles and says "Yes" to himself while he is still playing.

Is this an okay or not okay way to show his feelings? How is Tay'von feeling?

(put picture to the right)

Parker is feeling afraid because she hasn't finished her grandmother's birthday card.

Parker talks to an adult she trusts.

Is this an okay or not okay way to show her feelings?

How is Parker feeling?

(put picture to the right)

 **Strong Start Bulletin**

Dear Family,

This week, our **Strong Start** lesson extended ideas presented during last week's lesson. We reviewed the names of feelings: **happy, sad, angry, afraid, disgusted,** and **surprised.** We also reviewed those feelings that make us feel **good** or **not so good.** Throughout the lesson, Henry helped us understand that it is natural for everyone to experience all feelings. He also helped us to know **okay** and **not okay** ways to act on our feelings. We defined situations that make us experience certain feelings and examples of okay and not okay ways for handling the situations. Some examples that we discussed are listed in the table.

Feeling	Example	Okay	Not okay
Sad	Your dog runs away.	Telling a parent how you are feeling	Screaming and demanding a new pet
Angry	A friend borrows your toy car without asking.	Taking a deep breath and using nice words to tell your friend how you are feeling	Pulling the car out of your friend's hand

To better understand handling feelings, we read:

_____.

The following are great examples of relevant stories that you may want to read at home:

The Feelings Book by Todd Parr

The Chocolate-Covered-Cookie Tantrum by Deborah Blumenthal

Lots of Feelings by Shelley Rotner

At home, remind your child to do the following:

• Stop and identify the feeling he or she is experiencing.

• Determine whether it is a good or not so good feeling.

• Choose an okay way to act on that feeling.

Thanks for helping your child to apply what he or she has learned about identifying feelings. Be sure to congratulate your child each time he or she chooses an okay way to handle a difficult situation.

Fidelity Checklist

I. Review

☐ Review previous topics/main ideas. Prompt students to remember six basic feelings.

II. Introduction

☐ Communicate that students will talk more about feelings.

III. Read a Book from the Literature List

Book Title/Author: _____

☐ Help students to identify characters' feelings and behaviors.

☐ Use relevant questions to guide the discussion.

IV. Understanding Basic Emotions

☐ Revisit "If You're Happy and You Know It."

☐ Show feeling pictures and ask students to give examples of when they have had that feeling.

V. Identify Actions that Follow Feelings

☐ Convey that everyone has feelings and they are different at different times.

☐ Communicate that we can have more than one feeling at the same time.

☐ Communicate that it is important to talk about feelings.

☐ Convey that there are okay and not okay ways to show feelings.

VI. Okay and Not Okay Ways of Showing Feelings

☐ Use example situations to demonstrate okay and not okay ways of showing feelings.

☐ Engage children in a practice activity (stand up/sit down).

VII. Closure

☐ Remind students that it is all right to have any feeling.

☐ Review that there are different ways to show our feelings, **okay** and **not okay**.

Understanding Other People's Feelings

LESSON 4

SEL Competencies Addressed in This Lesson

Responsible decision making

Self-awareness

Relationship skills

Self-management

Social awareness

Teacher Notes

_____

_____

_____

_____

_____

_____

_____

_____

Purpose and Objectives

The purpose of this lesson is to teach students to identify others' feelings.

- Students will learn to use physical cues to understand how someone else is feeling.

Materials Needed

- ☐ Henry (stuffed animal mascot)
- ☐ Chart paper
- ☐ Supplements 4.1–4.6 (laminated cards)
- ☐ Book from the literature list (or one of your choice)
- ☐ Magnifying glass
- ☐ *Strong Start* Bulletin

Running Short on Time?

Consider segmenting the lesson. You may choose to introduce the lesson and read a book from the literature list with guiding questions. You may follow up with another lesson activity during which you have students play charades and complete a journal entry or extension activity.

Instructor Reflection

To best prepare for this lesson, think about the ways you decide how others are feeling. Do you look at a friend's facial expressions? Her physical stance? Do you listen carefully to what she is saying? How does understanding other people's feelings help you to interact with them? What are some situations in your classroom in which students don't always pay attention to each other's feelings? Are there situations in your classroom in which students feel different from one another?

Review

 2 MINS.   To activate prior knowledge, review and discuss previous topics and main ideas. Obtain three to five adequate ideas from the previous lesson. Make sure to provide feedback.

Sample Script

During our last meeting, we learned about naming our feelings and using okay ways to handle our feelings. Raise your hand if you can tell me an important idea we learned from this lesson.

Introduction

 1 MIN.   Communicate clearly the lesson's purpose and objectives.

Sample Script

Today, we will learn about understanding how other people feel. To help us understand how other people feel, we will learn how to notice what other people's bodies and faces look like when they are feeling different ways. This will make it easier for us to make friends and solve problems.

Optional Focusing Activity

Sample Script

Before we begin our lesson, let's practice calming our bodies and getting our brains ready to learn. Sit up straight, close your eyes, and take a big balloon breath.

Read a Book from the Literature List

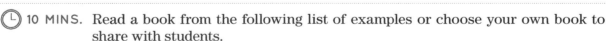 10 MINS.   Read a book from the following list of examples or choose your own book to share with students.

- *Harriet, You'll Drive Me Wild* by Mem Fox
- *Frog in the Middle* by Susanna Gretz
- *Chrysanthemum* by Kevin Henkes
- *The Rat and the Tiger* by Keiko Kasza
- *I Love My New Toy!* by Mo Willems

Be sure to point out all of the actions or ways in which the characters behave when they are acting on their feelings. Also note when different characters have different feelings in the same situation. Use the following questions to guide your discussion:

- What was one of the feelings the character had?

- Do you think it was a good or not so good feeling?

- What did the character look like when he or she was feeling that way?

- What did the character do when he or she was feeling that way?

- What clues did the character use to help him or her understand how other people were feeling?

- Were there any other times during this story when two people had different feelings in the same situation?

Name and Define Skill

🕐 1 MIN.   Convey the following main ideas to your students using your own words or the sample script provided:

- It might be possible to tell someone's feelings by looking for visual clues (like a detective).

- It is important to listen to others to find out how they are feeling.

Sample Script

Today, we're going to pretend to be detectives. Detectives are people who use special magnifying glasses to help them see things better and to find clues for solving mysteries. We are going to learn how we can be detectives to figure out how other people are feeling. The first clue we can look at is a person's face. The second clue we can look at is the rest of the person's body.

Modeling

🕐 10 MINS.

Model some feelings for the class or ask students to help you model feelings. Begin by showing one of the six basic emotion faces from Supplements 4.1–4.6 and describing how it looks. Then, model and list body language tied to each feeling.

Sample Script

[Show the picture of a happy face.] *This is happy. A happy face shows a smile.* [Model some happy body clues; e.g., smile, open arms, stand up straight, walk with head high, laugh.] *What body clues show you that I'm happy?*

[Show the picture of a sad face.] *This is sad. A sad face is not smiling. A tear may be rolling down a sad person's cheek.* [Model some sad body clues; e.g., frown, put head down, pull arms close to body, shuffle feet, cry.] *What body clues show you that I'm sad?*

Continue by having students identify the remaining faces from Supplements 4.1–4.6. For each feeling, act out the body clues (or have students help you), have students describe what your/their body(ies) looks like, and write down their responses. Examples of body clues include the following:

- *Happy*—smile, open arms, stand up straight, walk with head high, laugh
- *Sad*—frown, put head down, pull arms close to body, shuffle feet, cry
- *Angry*—turn red in the face, puff up lips, bare teeth, make threatening eye contact, clench fists, cross arms, take up space (e.g., hold arms away from body), walk quickly, shake
- *Scared*—open eyes wide, drop head, walk backward slowly, tremble
- *Disgusted*—stick tongue out, scrunch up eyes and nose, turn head away
- *Surprised*—open eyes wide, open mouth, step back, put hands on face

Model each feeling again. Have the students guess which feeling you are modeling. Practice with students until they can correctly identify five feelings and tell the clues that helped them to know. *Note:* You may need to spend more time on this if the class does not display mastery of interpreting the clues. Consider using student volunteers who can demonstrate mastery to model the feelings.

Closure

🕐 1 MIN.   Gather your students together and review the lesson objectives.

Sample Script

Today, we learned about ways we can tell how other people are feeling. We can be detectives and search for clues on others' faces and bodies. Recognizing how others are feeling will help us to be good friends and problem solvers. Be sure to practice your detective skills every day.

Applying What We Learned

Anticipate

Prior to social situations (e.g., partner/group activities, field trips, recess, transition times), remind students to be detectives and use visual clues to try to understand how other people feel.

Remind

If you notice a student is not using clues to understand how other people are feeling, remind him or her to do so. This reminder may be particularly useful in situations requiring problem solving (e.g., arguing over a toy, name-calling, telling on one another).

Acknowledge

If you notice your students using their detective skills and recognizing how other people are feeling, give them praise. Remember to be specific and name the particular skill you observed. For example, if you notice a student comforting another, you might say, "Mikey, I noticed that you used the clues that John was showing to understand how he is feeling. You are a great detective and friend!"

Extension Activity: Charades

Purpose and Objectives

Students will identify others' feelings using physical cues.

Materials

- ☐ Laminated cards depicting the six basic feelings (Supplements 4.1–4.6) *or*
- ☐ Large dice or beach ball with stripes of color

Procedure

1. Form small groups of students.
2. Using the laminated cards, or a large die with each number preassigned to represent a feeling, or a beach ball with each stripe of color preassigned to represent a feeling, have students act out the face and body clues that show the feeling.
3. Have the remaining students take turns guessing which feeling is being acted out.

Basic Feelings

Happy

Merrell's Strong Start—Pre-K: A Social and Emotional Learning Curriculum, Second Edition, by Sara A. Whitcomb and Danielle M. Parisi Damico.

Basic Feelings

Sad

Basic Feelings

Afraid

Basic Feelings

Angry

Basic Feelings

Surprised

Basic Feelings

Disgusted

Dear Family,

This week, our *Strong Start* lesson focused on *how to tell what others are feeling.* We talked about being detectives and searching for clues on others' faces and bodies. Recognizing how others are feeling will help us to be *good friends* and *problem solvers.* We had fun playing charades and guessing what feelings our classmates were modeling.

To better understand handling feelings, we read:

_____.

The following are great examples of relevant stories that you may want to read at home:

Chrysanthemum by Kevin Henkes

I Love My New Toy! by Mo Willems

Harriet, You'll Drive Me Wild by Mem Fox

At home, help your child to do the following:

• Be a detective.

• Look at the body clues of others.

Thanks for all that you do in helping your child to understand the feelings of others. Your support makes a difference in how your child uses the information presented in these lessons!

Fidelity Checklist

I. Review

☐ Refer to the previous lessons, **Understanding Your Feelings 1 and 2.**

☐ Review *okay* ways to handle *not so good* feelings.

II. Introduction

☐ Communicate that students will talk about understanding how other people feel.

☐ Communicate that students will learn to notice what other people's bodies and faces look like when people are feeling different ways.

III. Read a Book from the Literature List

Book Title/Author: _____

☐ Help students to identify characters' feelings and behaviors.

☐ Note how different characters have different feelings in the same situation.

☐ Use relevant questions to guide the discussion.

IV. Name and Define Skill/Modeling/Charades

☐ Explain how to tell another's feelings by looking for visual cues of face and body.

☐ Show faces from Supplements 4.1–4.6 and identify visual cues.

☐ Model body clues for various emotions and have students describe the clues.

☐ Act out feelings and have the students guess the feelings.

V. Closure

☐ Review ways to tell how others are feeling.

☐ Explain how to look for visual cues.

☐ Remind students that others may have different feelings and understanding them helps to be good friends.

LESSON 5
When You're Angry

SEL Competencies Addressed in This Lesson

Responsible decision making
Self-awareness
Relationship skills
Self-management
Social awareness

Teacher Notes

_____

_____

_____

_____

_____

_____

_____

_____

_____

Purpose and Objectives

The purpose of this lesson is to teach students about anger and helpful ways of handling anger.

- Students will accurately describe how their bodies feel when they are angry.

- Students will accurately list synonyms for the word *anger*.

- Students will identify situations that might make people angry.

- Students will understand Ways that Help and Ways that Hurt in handling their anger.

Materials Needed

- ☐ Henry (stuffed animal mascot)
- ☐ Chart paper
- ☐ Supplements 5.1–5.3 (laminated cards)
- ☐ Supplement 5.4 (stop sign)
- ☐ Book from the literature list (or one of your choice)
- ☐ Red crayons
- ☐ Drawing paper
- ☐ Crayons
- ☐ *Strong Start* Bulletin

Running Short on Time?

Consider breaking this lesson into segments. This could be done by introducing the topic and reading and reflecting on a book from the literature list. At another time, you could review Ways that Help in handling anger and have students complete one of the relevant activities suggested.

Instructor Reflection

To prepare for this lesson, think about how you experience anger. Where do you feel it in your body? How do you handle it? What are some healthy coping strategies that you might be able to share with your students? Think about challenging situations in your classroom, when you are likely to observe students feeling angry? How do they handle it? How do you work with them? How do you encourage students to manage their strong emotions?

Review

⏱ 2 MINS.   To activate prior knowledge, review and discuss previous topics and main ideas. Make sure to provide feedback.

Sample Script

During our last meeting, we learned how to be detectives and figure out how our friends are feeling. Raise your hand if you can guess how I am feeling [make a mad face]. How did you know I was feeling that way?

Introduction

⏱ 1 MIN.   Communicate clearly the lesson's purpose and objectives.

Sample Script

Today, we will talk about a feeling called anger. Anger is a normal feeling, and everybody feels angry sometimes. We will learn what anger looks like and when it might happen. We will also learn ways to deal with our anger so that we don't hurt ourselves or others.

Optional Focusing Activity

Sample Script

Before we read our story today, let's calm our bodies. Close your eyes and make your body still. Take a big balloon breath and get ready to use your listening ears.

Read a Book from the Literature List

🕐 10 MINS. Read a book from the following list of examples or choose your own to share with students.

- *The Anger Monster* by Jennifer Anzin
- *When Sophie Gets Angry—Really, Really Angry...* by Molly Bang
- *Josh's Smiley Faces: A Story About Anger* by Gina Ditta-Donahue
- *Just Being Me #1: I'm SO Mad!* by Robie H. Harris
- *Sometimes I'm Bombaloo* by Rachel Vail

Be sure to point out all of the actions or ways in which the characters behave when they are acting on their feelings. Use the following questions to guide your discussion:

- Which character was angry?
- Do you think it was a good or not good feeling?
- What did the character look like when he or she was angry?
- What did the character do when he or she was angry?
- Did the character use a Way that Hurts or a Way that Helps to handle his or her anger?

Show and Define Anger

🕐 5 MINS.
- Use Supplements 5.1 and 5.2 to show children pictures of different examples of angry faces.

- Be sure to point out facial features that depict anger (e.g., furrowed eyebrows, tight lips).

Sample Script

This is angry. Angry is a not so good feeling. What does angry look like in this picture? Raise your hand if you've ever felt angry. What did your body look or feel like?

- Have students share what their bodies felt like when they were angry. Examples include felt hot, had tight muscles, were shaky, or were teary.

- Help the students understand other words similar to anger. Examples include *anger*, *mad*, *furious*, and *upset*.

Ways of Handling Anger

🕐 10 MINS. Introduce the concept of Ways that Help and Ways that Hurt in handling anger.

Sample Script

Today, we've been talking about a feeling called anger. All people feel angry sometimes, and it's all right to feel angry. Most of the time, something happens to make us feel angry. This is called a spark. Sparks are little bits of fire that get hotter and hotter and turn into a big angry fire. Just like sparks start fire, something can "spark" our anger. There are things we can do to stop anger and keep it from spreading, and there are things we can do that spread the anger and hurt ourselves and others.

Act out the following scenario with Henry:

Henry: "Could I please go to my friend's house and play?"

Teacher: "Not today, Henry. We have to go to the grocery store. Maybe another time."

Discuss or show that when this happened, Henry's muscles got tight and he began to feel hot. Ask students, "What sparked Henry's anger in this situation? How did his body feel? What do you think Henry did?"

After students have shared their ideas for what Henry did when he was angry, explain that there are two ways that you can deal with your anger: Ways that Help and Ways that Hurt. Use Supplement 5.3 to introduce Ways that Help.

Sample Script

Henry felt really angry when he couldn't go to his friend's house. This was the spark. Because this happened a long time ago, Henry didn't know about Ways that Help and Ways that Hurt when handling his anger. In this situation, Henry stuck out his tongue, stomped his feet, and slammed the door to his room. When he was alone in the room, he kicked the wall. This kind of behavior is what I call Ways that Hurt. Henry stayed mad and wasn't acting nicely. When he got older and the same thing happened, he knew how to make himself feel better. He learned a special trick called Stop, Count, In, Out.

Stop, Count, In, Out strategy	
STOP	When you feel a spark, **stop** what you are doing.
COUNT	**Count** to 10.
IN	Take a deep breath **in**.
OUT	Breathe **out**.

These steps are all Ways that Help. Let's practice Stop, Count, In, Out together.

Use the following examples to assess children's understanding of the concept of Ways that Hurt and Ways that Help in handling anger. Have students stand up if it is a Way that Helps and stay sitting if it is a Way that Hurts.

Spark	What Henry does	Is it a Way that Helps or a Way that Hurts?
Henry's best friend did not want to share his new toy.	Henry took a deep breath and counted to 10.	It's a Way that Helps.
Henry's mom said he could not watch TV.	Henry yelled, "You're mean!"	It's a Way that Hurts.
Henry's block tower kept falling down before he was done building it.	Henry stopped what he was doing, counted to 10, and took a deep breath in and out.	It's a Way that Helps.
Henry did not get to be first in line when his class went outside for recess.	Henry pushed the line leader out of the way.	It's a Way that Hurts.

Closure

🕐 1 MIN. Gather your students together and review the lesson objectives.

Sample Script

Everyone feels angry sometimes, and there are many ways that we can handle our anger. It is important to use a Way that Helps so that we don't hurt ourselves or others.

Applying What We Learned

Anticipate

Tell your students to use Ways that Help (the Stop, Count, In, Out strategy) if something sparks their anger. Prompting them prior to recess, lunch, physical education periods, and partner activities might be particularly helpful.

Remind

If you find that a student is not dealing with his or her anger properly, remind him or her to handle the anger with a Way that Helps. Some students might benefit from your modeling the Stop, Count, In, Out strategy ("Watch me." Stop, count, breathe. "Your turn").

Acknowledge

If you see your students using Ways that Help to handle their anger, provide them with specific praise such as, "I like that you stopped and took a big, deep breath just then. I could tell that something had sparked your anger."

Extension Activity: Stop Sign

Complete at least one activity within 2 days of lesson implementation. Encourage students to cut out and color the stop sign depicted in Supplement 5.4. Have them glue the sign to a wooden craft stick and use it as a reminder to practice the Stop, Count, In, Out strategy.

Extension Activity: Bubble Snake

Purpose and Objectives

The purpose of the Bubble Snake activity is to encourage and practice the Stop, Count, In, Out strategy.

Materials

- ☐ Plastic bottle
- ☐ Scissors
- ☐ Sock or wash cloth
- ☐ Rubber band
- ☐ Dishwashing soap and water mixture (2 parts dishwashing soap plus 1 part water)
- ☐ Bowl

Procedure

1. Cut off the bottom fourth of any bottle. Decorate the bottle like an animal with goggle eyes, ears, whiskers, paint, or spikes for added effect.

2. Place the bottom of the bottle snugly into a washcloth or sock and rubber band it securely. Make sure the washcloth/sock is held flat against the end of the water bottle.

3. Dip the fabric end into the bowl with soapy water mixture. Allow mixture to soak into the cloth without become too saturated and heavy.

4. Blow into the other end of the bottle and watch the bubble snake emerge! Model for children how to Stop, Count, In, Out, strategy while using the bubble snake. *If the washcloth/sock becomes too wet, detach it, wring it out, and replace.*

I'm Angry!

Basic Feelings

Angry

The Stop, Count, In, Out Strategy

STOP		When you feel a spark, **stop** what you are doing.
COUNT	1 2 3 4 6 5 9 7 8 10	**Count** to 10.
IN		Take a deep breath **in**.
OUT		Breathe **out**.

Stop Sign

Dear Family,

This week, our **Strong Start** lesson focused on teaching students helpful ways of handling anger. We discussed how our bodies feel when we are angry, and we also listed synonyms for the word **anger.** Throughout the lesson, Henry helped us understand **Ways that Help** and **Ways that Hurt** in dealing with situations that make us angry. We shared ideas about appropriately stopping our **sparks** from turning into big, angry fires. Below is one strategy we practiced, the **Stop, Count, In, Out** strategy:

STOP	STOP	When you feel a spark, **stop** what you are doing.
COUNT	1 2 3 4 6 5 9 7 8 10	**Count** to 10.
IN		Take a deep breath **in.**
OUT		Breathe **out.**

To better understand handling anger, we read:

_____.

The following are great examples of relevant stories that you may want to read at home:

When Sophie Gets Angry—Really, Really Angry... by Molly Bang

Just Being Me #1: I'm SO Mad! by Robie H. Harris

Sometimes I'm Bombaloo by Rachel Vail

When your child becomes angry at home, remind him or her to do the following:

• Stop and identify the "spark."

• Count to 10, and breathe in and out.

• Act or behave in a Way that Helps.

At Home

Helping children to choose **Ways that Help** in handling anger is very important. If you see that your child is not making an appropriate choice for handling anger, help him or her to brainstorm a better way. If you notice your child making a great choice, be sure to praise his or her accomplishment (e.g., "I liked the way you took a breath when you started to get angry").

Fidelity Checklist

I. Review

- ☐ Refer to the previous lesson, **Understanding Other People's Feelings**.
- ☐ Remind students about being detectives to discover how friends are feeling.
- ☐ Refer to facial and body clues that can help us to understand how friends are feeling.

II. Introduction

- ☐ Communicate that students will talk about anger.
- ☐ Communicate that students will learn about what anger looks like.
- ☐ Communicate that students will learn about when anger might occur and how they can deal with their anger.

III. Read a Book from the Literature List

Book Title/Author: _____

- ☐ Help students to identify characters' feelings and behaviors.
- ☐ Use relevant questions to guide the discussion about anger.

IV. Show and Define Anger

- ☐ Use Supplements 5.1 and 5.2 or give examples of what angry faces look like.
- ☐ Point to facial features showing anger.
- ☐ Encourage students to share what their bodies feel like when they are angry.
- ☐ Encourage children to share times when they experienced anger.
- ☐ Brainstorm synonyms for anger.

V. Ways of Handling Anger

- ☐ Introduce **Ways that Help** and **Ways that Hurt** in handling anger.
- ☐ Act out a scenario in which Henry gets angry, and ask the students to identify his feelings and predict what he might do.
- ☐ Use a visual of Supplement 5.3 to show the **Stop, Count, In, Out** strategy.
- ☐ Provide multiple examples (**Ways that Help**) and nonexamples (**Ways that Hurt**) for handling anger.

VI. Closure

- ☐ Review with students that everyone feels angry sometimes.
- ☐ Remind students to use **Ways that Help** in handling anger.

LESSON 6

When You're Happy

SEL Competencies Addressed in This Lesson

Responsible decision making

Relationship skills

Self-awareness

Self-management

Social awareness

Teacher Notes

_____

_____

_____

_____

_____

_____

_____

_____

Purpose and Objectives

The purpose of this lesson is to teach students to feel happy and to comfort themselves when unhappy.

- Students will accurately identify features of people depicting the concept of happy.

- Students will describe how their bodies feel when they are happy.

- Students will accurately list synonyms for the word *happy*.

- Students will be exposed to the concept of Happy Talk.

Materials Needed

☐ Henry (stuffed animal mascot)

☐ A book from the literature list (or one of your choice)

☐ Chart paper

☐ Supplements 6.1–6.2 (PDF documents)

☐ Drawing paper

☐ Crayons

☐ *Strong Start* Bulletin

Running Short on Time?

Consider breaking this lesson into parts. You could introduce the concept and body cues depicting "happy" with a book from the literature list. During another session, you could introduce the concept of Happy Talk. As usual, extension activities can happen at any time prior to the next lesson.

Instructor Reflection

To best prepare for this lesson, think about how you make yourself feel better. What comforts do you have to help you cool down when mad or sad? What are situations in your classroom in which you notice students having negative thoughts? What do the students do? How do you help them feel better? How do you share happiness or joy with your students?

Review

 2 MINS. To activate prior knowledge, review and discuss previous topics and main ideas on the concept of anger from Lesson 5. Make sure to provide feedback and refer to the steps of the Stop, Count, In, Out strategy.

Sample Script

During our last meeting, we discussed feeling angry. Raise your hand if you can tell me Ways that Help you feel better when you are angry. How about a Way that Hurts?

Introduction

 1 MIN. Communicate clearly the lesson's purpose and objectives.

Sample Script

Today, we will talk about feeling happy. Everyone feels happy sometimes. It is a good feeling. Today, we will talk about what happy looks like and what happy feels like. We will think about how we can make ourselves feel happy when we are mad or sad.

Optional Focusing Activity

Sample Script

Before we get started, let's calm our bodies. Sit very still, close your eyes, and take a big balloon breath.

Read a Book from the Literature List

 10 MINS. Read a book from the following list of examples or choose your own book to share with students.

- *I Like Myself!* by Karen Beaumont
- *Fun Is a Feeling* by Chara M. Curtis
- *Stand Tall, Molly Lou Melon!* by Patty Lovell
- *Beautiful Oops!* by Barney Saltzberg
- *Super-Completely and Totally the Messiest* by Judith Viorst

As part of your reading, be sure to point out all of the actions or ways in which the characters behave when they are acting on their feelings. Use the following questions to guide your discussion:

- Which character was happy?

- Do you think it was a good or not so good feeling?

- What did the character look like when he or she was happy?

- What did the character do when he or she was happy?

Show and Define Happiness

⏱ 5 MINS.
- Use Supplements 6.1 and 6.2 to show children different examples of happy faces.

Sample Script

This is happy. Happy is a good feeling. What does happy look like in this picture? Raise your hand if you've ever felt happy. What did your body look or feel like?

- Point out facial features depicting happy in Supplements 6.1 and 6.2. Orient children toward smiling faces and similar expressions.

- Have students describe what their bodies felt like when they were happy. Examples include feeling comfortable, excited, and energetic.

- Help children understand words that are similar to *happy*. Examples might include *joy*, *glad*, and *cheerful*.

Happy Talk

⏱ 5 MINS.
Introduce the concept of Happy Talk. *Note:* This is a difficult concept for young children but is an important one that they can practice over time.

Sample Script

Today, we are going to learn about Happy Talk. Happy Talk is something that will help us to feel better when we are sad or mad. Remember, it is always okay to feel mad or sad. When we use Happy Talk, we can first Stop, Count, In, Out, and we can then remember that everything is going to be okay.

Act out the following scene with Henry to model an example and a nonexample of Happy Talk.

Scenario 1

Henry: "Hi. Could I play with your toy?"

Teacher: "Maybe later. I'm taking a turn with it right now."

Henry: "She never shares. I never get to play with her toys."

Scenario 2

Henry: "Hi. Could I play with your toy?"

Teacher: "Maybe later. I'm taking a turn with it right now."

Henry: [Henry counts to 10 and takes a deep breath.] "That's okay. I'll get a chance to play with it another time. I'll find something else to do."

Summarize that Happy Talk may include working to keep our bodies calm and finding another activity that will make us feel good on the inside.

Closure

🕐 1 MIN.   Gather your students together, and review the lesson objectives.

Sample Script

Today, we learned about feeling happy and Happy Talk. Everyone feels happy. It is a good feeling. If we use Happy Talk, we can make ourselves feel happy even if we are having not so good feelings.

Activity: Happy

🕐 10 MINS.   ***Complete this activity prior to the next lesson implementation.***

- Provide students with paper and crayons. Encourage them to draw a picture of their own face showing happiness. Help children to think about what their mouths, eyes, and eyebrows might look like when they are happy.

- Play Stand Up, Sit Down with students. Use the following examples, and have students stand up if Henry is using Happy Talk and sit down if he is not.

Problem	What Henry does	Is he using Happy Talk?
Henry did not get to watch TV before dinner like he usually does.	Henry took a breath. He said, "That's okay. Maybe I can watch TV later."	Yes
Henry wanted to ride his bike. His mom said no.	Henry yelled, "I am never going to ride my bike again!"	No
Henry was hungry for lunch, but his mom had to make it first. Henry had to wait.	Henry took a breath. He said, "That's okay. I'll play with LEGOs until lunch is ready."	Yes
Henry wanted to play with a friend who lived next door. His friend was not home.	Henry said, "He is not my friend, anyway! I don't ever want to play with him."	No

Applying What We Learned

Anticipate

Help your students to use Happy Talk when they are feeling bad. This may be particularly helpful before events that may cause negative feelings, such as partner activities, recess, and choice time.

Remind

If you find a student who is not using Happy Talk, tell him or her to take a deep breath and figure out a better way.

Acknowledge

If you are able to observe students using Happy Talk, be sure to applaud their application of this complex skill.

Extension Activity: Happy Rainbows

Purpose and Objectives

The purpose of this extension activity is for students to identify what makes them happy and to describe how their bodies feel when they are happy.

Materials

☐ Paper plates

☐ Cotton balls

☐ Rainbow-colored streamers or construction paper

☐ Glue

☐ Tape

Materials to prepare ahead of time:

- Cut paper plates in half.
- Cut streamers or construction paper to desired length.

Procedure

1. Students write or draw pictures on the streamers of what makes them happy.

2. Students write or draw pictures on the streamers of how their body feels when happy.

3. Students glue streamers onto the straight edge of a paper plate.

4. Students glue cotton balls onto paper plates.

I'm Happy!

Basic Feelings

Happy

Strong Start Bulletin

Dear Family,

This week, our **Strong Start** lesson focused on teaching students about **happiness.** We discussed how our bodies feel when we are happy and what actions or situations make us feel happy. We also listed synonyms for the word **happy.**

In this lesson, Henry helped us understand **Happy Talk.** We talked about how Happy Talk can make us feel better when we are sad or mad. When we use Happy Talk, we can stop, count, and take a breath and then remember everything is going to be okay.

To better understand happiness, we read:

_____.

The following are great examples of relevant stories that you may want to read at home:

Super-Completely and Totally the Messiest by Judith Viorst

Fun Is a Feeling by Chara M. Curtis

Stand Tall, Molly Lou Melon! by Patty Lovell

When your child becomes sad or mad at home, help him or her to do the following:

Remind him or her to remember the Happy Talk strategy noted above. This can be hard, and your child might need your help to think about a problem in a better way. For example, if your child mistakenly breaks a toy, an example of Happy Talk might be, "That's okay. I have other toys," rather than "What will I do? I have nothing to play with now."

Thanks for all of your support in helping your child to be a positive thinker!

Fidelity Checklist

I. Review

- ☐ Refer to the previous lesson, **When You're Angry.**
- ☐ Review **Ways that Help** and **Ways that Hurt** in dealing with anger.
- ☐ Refer to the steps of the **Stop, Count, In, Out** strategy.

II. Introduction

- ☐ Communicate that students will talk about feeling happy.
- ☐ Communicate that students will learn what their minds and bodies feel like when they are happy.
- ☐ Communicate that students will learn about how to make themselves feel happy when mad or sad.

III. Read a Book from the Literature List

Book Title/Author: _____

- ☐ Help students to identify characters' feelings and behaviors.
- ☐ Use relevant questions to guide the discussion about feeling happy.

IV. Show and Define Happiness

- ☐ Use Supplements 6.1 and 6.2 or give examples of what happy faces look like.
- ☐ Encourage students to share what their bodies feel like when they are happy.
- ☐ Encourage children to share times when they felt happy.
- ☐ Have each student generate a list of words that make him or her think of happiness.

V. Happy Talk

- ☐ Introduce the concept of *Happy Talk.*
- ☐ Explain to students that positive thinking can make them feel better when they experience feelings that are not good. Provide examples.
- ☐ Describe how in Happy Talk children can first use Stop, Count, In, Out and then remind themselves that everything is going to be okay.
- ☐ Model (use Henry to role play) an example and nonexample of using Happy Talk.

VI. Closure

- ☐ Review with students that everyone feels happy sometimes.
- ☐ Remind students to use **Positive Thinking** when they are having not so good feelings.

LESSON 7

When You're Worried

Teacher Notes

_____

_____

_____

_____

_____

_____

_____

_____

Purpose and Objectives

The purpose of this lesson is to teach students to recognize and manage anxiety, worry, and fear.

- Students will accurately describe how their bodies feel when they are worried.

- Students will accurately list synonyms for the word _worried_.

- Students will identify situations that might make people worried.

- Students will try a basic relaxation technique.

Materials Needed

- ☐ Henry (stuffed animal mascot)
- ☐ Book from the literature list (or one of your choice)
- ☐ Chart paper
- ☐ Supplements 7.1–7.2 (PDF documents)
- ☐ _Strong Start_ Bulletin

Running Short on Time?

Consider breaking this lesson into parts. You could introduce the concept of "worry" with a book from the literature list, and then help students identify scenarios when they have felt worried. During another session, you could introduce the concept of Happy Talk.

Instructor Reflection

To best prepare for this lesson, think about how you experience worry or anxiety. Do you have strategies for comforting yourself? Do you get stuck thinking about the worry over and over? Consider situations in your classroom in which you have observed students experiencing worry. How do they respond? How have you helped them to let go of worries?

Review

🕐 **2 MINS.** To activate prior knowledge, review and discuss previous topics and main ideas from Lesson 6, When You're Happy. Make sure to provide feedback.

Sample Script

During our last meeting, we learned about Happy Talk. Raise your hand if you can tell me an important idea we learned from this lesson.

Introduction

🕐 **1 MIN.** Communicate clearly the lesson's purpose and objectives.

Sample Script

Today, we will talk about feeling worried. Feeling worried is a not so good feeling, but everyone feels worried sometimes. It's normal. Feeling worried is sometimes like feeling scared. We will learn how our bodies are when we are worried and think about when we might worry. We will also learn ways to deal with our worries so that we don't feel worried all the time.

Optional Focusing Activity

Sample Script

Before we get started learning about worries, let's calm our bodies. Close your eyes, make your body still and soft, and take a big balloon breath.

Read a Book from the Literature List

🕐 **10 MINS.** Read a book from the following list of examples or choose your own to share with students.

- *Even if I Did Something Awful* by Barbara Shook Hazen
- *Wemberly Worried* by Kevin Henkes
- *The Kissing Hand* by Audrey Penn

- *The Good-Bye Book* by Judith Viorst
- *Owl Babies* by Martin Waddell

Be sure to point out all of the actions or ways in which the characters behave when they are acting on their feelings. Use the following questions to guide your discussion:

- Which character was worried?
- Do you think it was a good or not so good feeling?
- What did the character look like when he or she was worried?
- What did the character do when he or she was worried?

Show and Define Worry

 5 MINS.

- Use Supplement 7.1 to show children different examples of worried faces.

Sample Script

This is worried. Worried can be a not so good feeling. What does worried look like in this picture? Raise your hand if you've ever felt worried. What did your body look or feel like?

- Have students share what their bodies feel like when they are worried. Examples include stomach ache, shaky hands and bodies, clenched fists, clenched teeth, and tightened muscles.

- Help children understand words similar to *worry*. Examples include *bothered*, *troubled*, *concerned*, *nervous*, and *uneasy*.

Letting Go of Worries

 5 MINS.

Explain to your students that you will be learning about what it is like to be worried and that Henry will help you with this.

Sample Script

Today, we've been talking about feeling worried. When we are worried, we often have a stomach ache or maybe our muscles feel tight. When we feel this way, it can be hard to stop ourselves. We think about our worry all the time. One time, Henry felt very worried. His mom was supposed to pick him up from school but she was late. Henry's stomach hurt, and he kept thinking, "Where could she be? Where could she be?" How do you think Henry could have comforted himself?

Display Supplement 7.2 and explain how the Stop, Count, In, Out strategy and Happy Talk can be helpful tools for letting go of worries.

Sample Script

When you use Happy Talk, you can help yourself feel better by naming your worry and talking to someone you trust about your worry. You might learn that this is not the worst problem in the whole world, and it can be fixed. You could also remember a time when something like this happened before and it turned out okay. Your Happy Talk might be, "It's all going to be okay."

The Stop, Count, In, Out strategy	
STOP	When you feel a spark, **stop** what you are doing.
COUNT	**Count** to 10.
IN	Take a deep breath **in.**
OUT	Breathe **out.**

Act out the following scenario with Henry.

Henry: "Where could she be? I know my mom is supposed to be here to pick me up!" [Henry takes a deep breath and says to the teacher] "I am worried because my mom is late."

Teacher: "I understand that might make you nervous, but do you remember what happened when your mom was late once before?"

Henry: "Oh, yeah. I got to play with my friends at school for a little longer. It was fun! Mom was just a little late because she had to get gas for her car. She picked me up as soon as she could. It is all okay."

Closure

🕐 1 MIN.   Gather your students together and review the lesson objectives.

Sample Script

Today, we talked about feeling worried. Everyone feels worried sometimes, and it does not feel good. If you're feeling worried, think about Happy Talk and the Stop, Count, In, Out strategy. Try to comfort yourself and make your body feel calm.

Activity: Relaxation Exercise

🕐 10 MINS.   *Complete this activity prior to the next lesson implementation.*

- Provide students with another strategy for letting go of worries.

Sample Script

Another way to help us let go of our worries is to focus on making our bodies feel better. We are going to practice a special exercise. It might feel silly at first, but if you follow all of my directions, your body will feel more calm.

- Have students find a quiet, comfortable place.

- Ask them to sit or lie quietly. Dim the lights if possible.

- Say, "Close your eyes. Take deep breaths. Breathe in and out slowly."

- Have students tighten their muscles, group by group. Then, ask them to loosen their muscles and make their bodies calm.

- Say, "Think about your favorite place, a place that makes you feel happy and calm."

- Say, "Sit quietly for a few minutes and continue breathing deeply and thinking about your happy place."

Applying What We Learned

Anticipate

Whenever appropriate, remind students to identify times when their bodies may be showing them that they are feeling worried. Prior to situations that may cause worry, such as interruptions in daily routines, remind students to be on the lookout for body clues such as stomach aches, tense muscles, and shaky bodies. Remind them to use the Stop, Count, In, Out strategy to help let go of worries.

Remind

If you find a student who is showing physical signs of worry, remind the student to use strategies that will help his or her body to feel calm.

Acknowledge

When you observe students who name their worries or notice students trying to keep a calm body, specify the strategy and compliment them for using it.

Extension Activity: Calming Bags

Purpose and Objectives

The purpose of this extension activity is to teach students to recognize and manage anxiety, worry, and fear by trying a basic relaxation technique. Children can make and then keep the calming bag. Touching or squeezing the bag might provide sensory input to help children relax and might also serve as a prompt to relax and let go of worries.

Materials

☐ Zip-closure plastic storage bags, or bottles

☐ Clear packing tape or duct tape

☐ Hair gel or a similar viscous liquid

☐ Food coloring

☐ Beads, puff balls, google eyes, dice, ribbon, buttons, sand, alphabet letters, confetti, glitter, shells, cars, LEGOs, stickers

Procedure

1. Fill baggie about one third full of hair gel.

2. Add coloring and any items.

3. Fold the bag over, pushing air out, sealing it, and taping it.

4. Add stickers to the outside of the bag.

5. Place inside another bag, seal it, and tape it.

I'm Worried!

The Stop, Count, In, Out Strategy

STOP		When you feel a spark, **stop** what you are doing.
COUNT	1 2 3 4 6 5 9 7 8 10	**Count** to 10.
IN		Take a deep breath **in**.
OUT		Breathe **out**.

 Strong Start **Bulletin**

Dear Family,

This week, our **Strong Start** lesson focused on teaching students helpful ways of **handling worries.** We discussed how our bodies feel when we are worried, and we also listed synonyms for the word **worry.** Throughout the lesson, Henry helped us understand strategies for letting go of our worries. He taught us to use the **Stop, Count, In, Out strategy** (outlined below) to make us feel better.

The Stop, Count, In, Out Strategy		
STOP	STOP	When you feel a spark, **stop** what you are doing.
COUNT	1 2 3 4 6 5 9 7 8 10	**Count** to 10.
IN		Take a deep breath **in.**
OUT		Breathe **out.**

To better understand our worries, we read:

_____. At Home

The following are great examples of relevant stories that you may want to read at home:

Wemberly Worried by Kevin Henkes

The Kissing Hand by Audrey Penn

The Good-Bye Book by Judith Viorst

When your child becomes worried at home, encourage him or her to let go by using the strategy above and by taking time to do the following:

• Name his or her worry.

• Talk about it.

• Understand that it is not necessarily the worst problem and can likely be fixed.

• Think about a time when something like this happened before and turned out okay.

All children worry sometimes, and helping them to understand their worries is important. Thanks for your support in this endeavor!

Fidelity Checklist

I. Review

☐ Refer to the previous lesson, **When You're Happy.**

☐ Review **positive (happy) thinking.**

II. Introduction

☐ Communicate that students will talk about feeling worried.

☐ Communicate that everyone feels worried sometimes.

☐ Communicate that students will learn about how to deal with worries.

III. Read a Book from the Literature List

Book Title/Author: _____

☐ Help students to identify characters' feelings and behaviors.

☐ Use relevant questions to guide the discussion about feeling worried.

IV. Show and Define Worry

☐ Show pictures or give examples of what worried faces look like.

☐ Encourage students to share what their bodies feel like when they are worried.

☐ Brainstorm synonyms for worry.

V. Letting Go of Worries

☐ Show students Supplement 7.2 and talk about how **Happy Talk** and **Stop, Count, In, Out** strategies help us to let go of worries.

☐ Model how to "let go of worries" with Henry.

VI. Closure

☐ Review with students that everyone feels worried sometimes.

☐ Remind students to use **Happy Talk** and **Stop, Count, In, Out** strategies to let go of worries.

LESSON 8

Being a Good Friend

SEL Competencies Addressed in This Lesson

Purpose and Objectives

The purpose of this lesson is to teach students basic communication and friendship-making skills.

- Students will discriminate between a nice voice and a not so nice voice.

- Students will practice listening skills.

- Students will learn the importance of eye contact and body language when relating with others.

- Students will learn the skills needed to initiate and maintain friendships.

Teacher Notes

_____

_____

_____

_____

_____

_____

_____

_____

Materials Needed

☐ Henry (stuffed animal mascot)

☐ A book from the literature list (or one of your choice)

☐ Supplement 8.1 (PDF document)

☐ Drawing paper

☐ Crayons

☐ *Strong Start* Bulletin

Running Short on Time?

Consider breaking the lesson into parts. During one part, you might read a book and discuss friendship globally. During another part, you might engage students in a discussion about using a nice voice and taking notice of others. You might follow with one of the activity ideas provided.

Instructor Reflection

To prepare for this lesson, consider your own friendships. How do you show friends that you are listening and that you care? How do you share or work with others? What do you notice about friendships in your classroom? How do students talk and listen to one another? How do you help students to learn these skills?

Review

🕒 2 MINS. To activate prior knowledge, review and discuss previous topics and main ideas. Obtain one to two adequate ideas from Lesson 4 on understanding others' feelings. Make sure to provide feedback.

Sample Script

During our last meeting, we learned about understanding our worries. Raise your hand if you can tell me an important idea we learned from this lesson.

Introduction

🕒 1 MIN. Communicate clearly the lesson's purpose and objectives.

Sample Script

Today, we will be learning about how to be a good friend. We will learn how to use our words, eyes, ears, and bodies to help us make friends. We will also talk about how to work together with friends.

Optional Focusing Activity

Sample Script

Before we get started, let's calm our bodies. We can sit crisscross and keep our backs straight like a stick. Close your eyes and take three big balloon breaths in and out.

Read a Book from the Literature List

🕒 10 MINS. Read a book from the following list of examples, or choose your own book to share with students.

- *We Are Best Friends* by Aliki
- *Do You Want to Be My Friend?* by Eric Carle
- *How To Grow a Friend* by Sara Gillingham
- *Enemy Pie* by Derek Munson
- *Yo! Yes?* by Chris Raschka

Be sure to point out all of the actions or ways in which the characters behave as good friends. Use the following questions to guide your discussion:

- Which people were friends in the story?

- How did they talk to each other?

- How did they become friends?

- What were some of the things they did together?

Talking and Listening

🕒 5 MINS.   Communicate the necessary body clues for talking nicely, and give examples and nonexamples of a friendly voice.

Sample Script

Today, we're going to learn about how friends should talk and listen to each other. When we talk to others, we should smile and use a nice voice. A nice voice is soft and gentle and not loud like yelling.

Use Henry to model an example and a nonexample of a nice voice.

Nonexample

Henry: [Yelling and using a not nice voice] "Hey! Let me play now!"

Example

Henry: [Using a nice voice] "Hi there. May I play with you?"

Communicate the necessary body clues for listening, and give examples and nonexamples of being a good listener.

Sample Script

When friends talk to each other, they use a nice voice. Friends are also good listeners. When we listen, we use our eyes, ears, and bodies. We look at the person who is talking, we keep calm bodies, and we hear what the person is saying.

Model an example and a nonexample of being a good listener.

Nonexample

Henry: "Hi there. May I play with you?"

Teacher: [Continues to play and ignores Henry]

Example

Henry: "Hi there. May I play with you?"

Teacher: [Looking toward Henry, smiles and says] "Sure, Henry. I'd love to have you join in the game!"

Approaching Others and Sharing

🕒 5 MINS.   Explain how to begin a friendship or an activity with friends. *Note:* It is important to remember that there are cultural differences in social interaction. In some cultures, eye contact may not be an appropriate way to communicate. Please use other more appropriate examples as you see fit.

Sample Script

When we're friends, we listen to each other and use nice voices. Part of being a good friend is noticing others as they come up to you and showing them that you care. When you move close to one another and smile and say hi, you're taking notice. When you ask someone to play, you show that you care and want to be a friend. Sometimes, it can be hard to know how to join in with others or ask someone to play. Let's make a list of different things we can do or say to show others that we want to be friends.

Provide children with examples such as, "Hi, do you want to play?" or "Henry, have you ever played with this toy before? Want to give it a try?" Gather further appropriate examples from children.

Explain the importance of maintaining friendships through sharing and working together. Elicit from the students some examples of sharing and working together. If someone provides an idea that is not appropriate, be sure to provide some corrective feedback and give examples of some better ways to show how to be a friend.

Sample Script

It is important to always treat our friends in a nice way so that we can stay friends. We should make sure to listen to our friends and use a nice voice. It is also important to share and to work together. Sometimes, two people will want to use the same thing or play with the same toy. Friends work together, use nice talk, and listen to each other to figure out a way to both be happy.

Act out the following scenario with Henry:

Henry: "I want to use the purple marker."

Teacher: "That is the one I wanted to use, too. What should we do?"

Henry: "I know. First, you can use it, and when you are finished with it, you can give it to me."

Teacher: "Great idea. Thanks, Henry!"

Closure

🕒 1 MIN.   Gather your students together and review the lesson objectives.

Sample Script

Today, we learned how to be a good friend. We can use our words, eyes, ears, and bodies to help us make friends. It is also important for us to treat our friends nicely and work together so that we can stay friends.

Activity: Make a Class Book

⏰ 10 MINS. *Complete this activity within 2 days of lesson implementation.*

As a closure activity, have the students each make a page for a class book. Use Supplement 8.1 and ask students to dictate what a good friend does. Then, have them draw pictures. If time permits and students are willing, have a few children share their drawings with the class.

Applying What We Learned

Anticipate

Encourage your students to look and listen to one another and to use nice voices. Prompt them prior to social times (e.g., recess, lunch, free play, partner activities). Anticipate situations that might occur within your classroom, and consider acting out scenarios with Henry prior to those situations.

Remind

If you notice a student who is not using his or her friendship skills, remind him or her to listen, to use a nice voice, to share, and to work together. It might be necessary at first for you to role-play what these skills look like when providing these reminders.

Acknowledge

If you see your students using their friendship skills, be sure to recognize their efforts (e.g., "I like how you asked Mary to play. You used a nice voice and had a smile on your face!").

Extension Activity: Compliment Circle

Purpose and Objectives

The purpose of this activity is to teach compliments and allow students to practice communicating. Students will demonstrate their ability to listen, to use a nice voice with appropriate eye contact, and to use body language to relate to others.

Materials

☐ List of character traits: sharing, caring, helpful, kind, fun, listening

Procedure

1. Introduce the "compliment circle."

2. Teach character traits.

3. Have students compliment the person next to them.

4. Closing

Variation: The teacher can say an additional compliment for each student to model and provide a character compliment to support the child.

What Does a Good Friend Do?

STRONG KIDS™

A good friend:

_____

_____

_____

_____

_____

Strong Start Bulletin

Dear Family,

This week, our *Strong Start* lesson focused on how to be a *good friend.* We discussed how friends should talk with a *nice voice* and actively listen to each other by maintaining eye contact, keeping a calm body, and hearing what others have to say. Part of being a good friend also includes noticing others as they approach and showing them that we care. Finally, we talked about how important it is to *share* and *work together* with our friends. The lesson was complete when children compiled a book of words and pictures depicting good friends.

To better understand handling feelings, we read:

_____.

At Home

The following are great examples of relevant stories that you may want to read at home:

Frog and Toad Together by Arnold Lobel

The Giving Tree by Shel Silverstein

George and Martha by James Marshall

At home, help your child to do the following:

• Use a nice voice.

• Use eyes, ears, and bodies to show good listening.

• Take notice of others by saying hi or inviting them to play.

• Take turns and share.

Making and keeping friends can be hard work. Thanks for supporting your child as he or she learns these important skills. Your guidance and acknowledgment will help your child to be a good friend to others.

Fidelity Checklist

I. Review

- ☐ Refer to the previous lesson, **When You're Worried.**
- ☐ Review strategies for using Happy Talk and letting go of worries.

II. Introduction

- ☐ Communicate that students will talk about being good friends.
- ☐ Communicate that students will learn about how to use words, eyes, ears, and bodies to help make friends.

III. Read a Book from the Literature List

Book Title/Author:_____

- ☐ Help students to identify characters' behaviors as they became friends.
- ☐ Use relevant questions to guide the discussion about being a good friend.

IV. Talking and Listening

- ☐ Encourage students to use a nice voice (soft and gentle) when talking to friends.
- ☐ Encourage students to use their eyes, ears, and bodies to show that they are listening to friends.
- ☐ Use Henry to model examples and nonexamples of using a nice voice and being a good listener.

V. Approaching Others

- ☐ Explain how to begin a friendship or activity with friends.
- ☐ Brainstorm a list of ways to show others that you want to be a friend.

VI. Sharing and Working Together/Activity

- ☐ Explain that good friends share and work together.
- ☐ Model sharing with Henry.

VII. Closure

- ☐ Review concepts related to being a good friend (e.g., using nice voices, listening ears, kind words).
- ☐ Review that being a good friend makes it easier to work together and share.

133

LESSON 9

Solving People Problems

SEL Competencies Addressed in This Lesson

- Responsible decision making
- Self-awareness
- Relationship skills
- Self-management
- Social awareness

Teacher Notes

_____

_____

_____

_____

_____

_____

_____

_____

_____

Purpose and Objectives

The purpose of this lesson is to teach students to solve problems with others.

- Students will describe problems that might occur between friends.
- Students will review Ways that Help in dealing with anger.
- Students will review Happy Talk.
- Students will practice problem-solving strategies.

Materials Needed

- ☐ Henry (stuffed animal mascot)
- ☐ Supplement 9.1 (laminated card)
- ☐ A book from the literature list (or one of your choice)
- ☐ *Strong Start* Bulletin

Running Short on Time?

Consider breaking this lesson into parts. You may read a book from the literature list and give initial examples of problem solving during one period. At another time, you may consider giving the class opportunities to practice identifying further examples and nonexamples of "making it better."

Instructor Reflection

To prepare for this lesson, consider some of the strategies that you use when you are faced with interpersonal conflict.

Do you take some space and work to resolve the conflict when you feel calm? Do you engage in brainstorming solutions? Are you able to assert yourself while being empathic to another's needs? What does problem solving look like in your classroom? How do you help students to work through a conflict?

Review

 2 MINS. To activate prior knowledge, review and discuss previous topics and main ideas from Lesson 8, Being a Good Friend. Make sure to provide feedback, and refer to the use of nice voices, good listening, and eye contact.

Sample Script

During our last meeting, we discussed how to be a friend. Raise your hand if you can tell me one way that you might be a friend.

Introduction

🕐 1 MIN. Communicate clearly the lesson's purpose and objectives.

Sample Script

Today, we will talk about solving problems with others. Everyone has problems sometimes. Problems often happen when we don't agree or when we want to do something that our friends don't. Problems often make us feel mad or sad, and these are not so good feelings. Today, we will think about how we can make ourselves feel happy when we are mad or sad and how we can solve problems when they happen.

Optional Focusing Activity

Sample Script

Before we begin our lesson, let's get into our ready position. Sit up nice and straight, close your eyes, and let's try our balloon breaths. Take three big breaths.

Read a Book from the Literature List

 🕐 10 MINS. Read a book from the following list of examples, or choose your own book to share with students.

- *Move Over, Twerp* by Martha Alexander
- *I Can't Wait* by Elizabeth Crary
- *I'm Frustrated* by Elizabeth Crary
- *Bet You Can't* by Penny Dale
- *Chester's Way* by Kevin Henkes
- *Words Are Not for Hurting* by Elizabeth Verdick and Marieka Heinlen

Be sure to point out all of the actions or ways in which the characters behave when they are acting on their feelings. Use the following questions to guide your discussion:

- What was one of the feelings the character had?

- Do you think it was a good or not so good feeling?

- What was the problem?

- What did the character do when he or she was faced with a problem?

- How did the character solve his or her problem?

Types of People Problems

 10 MINS. Explain the idea of disagreement, or *people problems*, and use Henry to provide an example.

Sample Script

We have a problem when we don't agree or when we want to do something our friends don't. Problems often make us feel sad or mad, and these are not so good feelings.

   For example, one time, Henry was excited for a playdate at his friend's house because his friend has really cool LEGOs. When Henry arrived, he had a problem, and it was a not so good feeling.

Act out the following scenario with Henry:

Henry: "Hi there. I am so excited for our playdate. I was hoping that we could play with your LEGOs."

Friend: "Sorry, Henry, but I want to paint with my new paint set."

- Have students share problems they have encountered. Possible examples include arguing over toys, not taking turns, cutting in line, and not working together on a group activity.

- Ensure respectful sharing by reminding students not to use names and to remember to use nice words.

Review Ways that Help and Happy Talk

 5 MINS. Review the concept of Ways that Help (Supplement 9.1) for handling anger and using Happy Talk.

Sample Script

When we have a problem, we usually feel mad or sad. It is important for us to remember Ways that Help us feel better when we are angry.

Sample Script

It is also important to remember Happy Talk. Happy Talk will help us to feel better when we have a problem. Remember, when we use Happy Talk, we feel better and have the feeling that everything is going to be okay. When we use Happy Talk, we can name how we are feeling and tell someone we trust. When we don't use Happy Talk, we might get stuck feeling sad or mad.

Comforting Yourself and Solving People Problems

🕐 10 MINS. Introduce strategies for solving problems.

- Use the Stop, Count, In, Out strategy.
- Use Happy Talk.
- Be a friend.
- Make it better.

Sample Script

When a problem sparks a not so good feeling, we need to Stop, Count, In, Out. After taking a deep breath, we need to continue to comfort ourselves by remembering how to be a friend. When we use nice voices, listen, and look at our friends, it will be easier for us to tell them what is wrong and fix the problem. It will be easier for us to "make it better."

Stop, Count, In, Out strategy	
STOP	When you feel stuck with a not so good feeling, **stop** what you are doing.
COUNT	**Count** to 10.
IN	Take a deep breath **in**.
OUT	Breathe **out**.

Act out the following scenarios with Henry.

Nonexample of "making it better":

Henry: "I wanted to play with LEGOs, and I am not going to play with you again if we don't play with LEGOs."

Friend: [Begins to cry] "Fine. You are not my friend anymore."

Example of "making it better":

Henry: [Uses the Stop, Count, In, Out strategy] "Hmm. I really wanted to play with LEGOs, and you want to paint. That makes me feeel a little mad on the inside."

Friend: "Maybe we could make it better. We could ask my mom to help fix the problem, or we could decide to play something else."

Henry: "I know! First, we could paint, and then we could play with LEGOs!"

Friend: "Great idea, Henry!"

Make sure children understand the difference between the scenarios, and encourage them to remember to use strategies for fixing problems.

Closure

 1 MIN. Gather your students together and review the lesson objectives.

Sample Script

Today, we learned about fixing problems we have with others. We learned to "make it better." Everyone has problems sometimes, and these problems often make us have not so good feelings. We can use the Stop, Count, In, Out strategy and Happy Talk to solve problems with others.

Activity: Role Play

10 MINS. ***Complete this activity within 2 days of lesson implementation.***

To help your students build fluency in solving people problems, use Henry to act out more nonexamples of problem solving similar to the one provided in the lesson. After you have acted out the nonexample, have students come up and act out how they might fix the problem. Be sure to praise students' efforts to use Ways that Help and Happy Talk. Try to use scenarios that are relevant to daily situations that arise in your classroom. Example scenarios are provided in the chart. Use topics such as sharing, cleaning up, following rules during a game, and choosing a friend to sit next to.

Problem	What happens	Making it better
Henry wants a turn on the swings, but they are all being used.	Henry yells loudly at you, "It's my turn!"	Henry takes a deep breath and says to you, "Could I have a turn in a few minutes?"
You and Henry are playing with blocks, and it is clean-up time.	Henry walks away and does not help you clean up.	You take a breath and use a nice voice to say, "Henry, you played this game with me. Will you help me clean up?"
You and Henry are coloring. You both want to use the green crayon.	You and Henry both grab at the crayon and yell, "It's mine!"	You decide to let Henry use it first and choose a different part of the picture to work on. Henry gives you the green crayon when he is done with it.

Applying What We Learned

Anticipate

Encourage your students to be problem solvers when they disagree with one another. Remind them to use the Stop, Count, In, Out strategy and Happy Talk when a problem arises. Be sure to prompt them before events during which problems might arise (e.g., a difficult board game, a game with a lot of rules, a group project).

Remind

If you notice a student who is not problem solving, remind him or her to use the strategies learned in class. You might have to break the problem-solving process into manageable parts. For example, first encourage the student to engage in the Stop, Count, In, Out strategy, and then prompt him or her to use Happy Talk and be a friend in order to help solve the problem.

Acknowledge

If you see your students problem solving, be sure to give specific praise (e.g., "I really liked that you stopped and took a breath and then decided to take turns with that game. Great problem solving!").

Extension Activity: "Make It Better" Jar

Purpose and Objectives

The purpose of this extension activity is to teach students to solve problems with others and to practice problem-solving strategies.

Materials

☐ Container labeled "Make It Better"

☐ Examples of classroom-specific challenges

Procedure

1. Record types of problems on slips of paper and place them in the jar.

2. Take out a piece of paper and read the problem out loud.

3. Discuss or act out solutions, and chart or record the solutions.

4. (This could be added to your weekly classroom routine.)

The Stop, Count, In, Out Strategy

STOP		When you feel a spark, **stop** what you are doing.
COUNT		**Count** to 10.
IN		Take a deep breath **in**.
OUT		Breathe **out**.

Dear Family,

This week, our **Strong Start** lesson focused on how to **solve problems** with others. We brainstormed a list of potential problems we might have with our peers. Then, we talked about the actions we might take when problems arise. We learned that we could use the **Stop, Count, In, Out breathing strategy** when we get angry, and after taking a deep breath, we could comfort ourselves by remembering how to be a friend. When we use nice voices, listen, and look at friends, it will be easier to work together and share ideas for fixing the problem so that we all feel better. We practiced our **problem-solving or "making it better" skills** by role-playing with classmates. The following table reflects an example of problem-solving behavior.

Problem	What Henry does after Stop, Count, In, Out	Is he making it better or not making it better?
Henry wants to play with LEGOs, but his friend wants to paint.	Henry and his friend decide to paint for a while and then play LEGOs.	He is making it better.
Henry wants to play with LEGOs, but his friend wants to paint.	Henry does not listen to his friend's ideas and says, "I'm not going to play with you anymore."	He is not making it better.

To better understand how to solve people problems, we read:

_____

The following are great examples of relevant stories that you may want to read at home:

Chester's Way by Kevin Henkes

I'm Frustrated by Elizabeth Crary

I Can't Wait by Elizabeth Crary

When problems arise at home, help your child to do the following:

• Stop and take a deep breath.

• Be a friend by looking at and listening to others.

• Work with others to brainstorm a solution.

If you see your child problem solving, be sure to congratulate his or her efforts (e.g., "I really liked that you stopped and took a breath and then decided to take turns with that game. Great job making it better!"). Thanks again for your support!

Fidelity Checklist

I. Review

- ☐ Refer to the previous lesson, **Being a Good Friend.**
- ☐ Question students on skills they need to be a friend.

II. Introduction

- ☐ Communicate that everyone has problems.
- ☐ Communicate that when we disagree, we may feel mad or sad.
- ☐ Explain that we will learn to solve problems and make ourselves feel happy.

III. Read a Book from the Literature List

Book Title/Author: _____

- ☐ Help students to identify characters' feelings and behaviors.
- ☐ Use relevant questions to guide the discussion about how to solve problems.

IV. Define Types of People Problems

- ☐ Explain the idea of disagreement or "people problems."
- ☐ Model a problem scenario with Henry.
- ☐ Encourage students to share problems they have had with others.

V. Comforting Yourself/Solving Problems

- ☐ Use Supplement 9.1 to review the idea that **Happy Talk** and **Stop, Count, In, Out** strategies help us feel better when we have a problem.
- ☐ Communicate the importance of being a friend when brainstorming solutions.
- ☐ Act out examples with Henry to deepen students' understanding of problem solving.

VI. Closure

- ☐ Review with students that everyone has problems sometimes.
- ☐ Remind students to use **Happy Talk** and **Stop, Count, In, Out** strategies to solve problems.

Finishing UP!

SEL Competencies Addressed in This Lesson

Responsible decision making · Self-awareness · Relationship skills · Self-management · Social awareness

Teacher Notes

_____

_____

_____

_____

_____

_____

_____

_____

Purpose and Objectives

The purpose of this lesson is to review the major concepts and skills in the *Strong Start—Pre-K* curriculum.

- Students will name feelings and describe okay and not okay ways of expressing feelings.

- Students will review Happy Talk and the Stop, Count, In, Out strategy.

Materials Needed

- ☐ Henry (stuffed animal mascot)
- ☐ Supplements 10.1–10.3 (laminated cards)
- ☐ Books from the literature list
- ☐ *Strong Start* Bulletin

Running Short on Time?

This is a review lesson, and you can make it longer or shorter if necessary. If you want to do an extensive review of topics, consider segmenting the lesson into parts. During one, you might review the topics covered in *Strong Start—Pre-K*, and during another, you might read a book from the literature list and create a *Strong Start* toolbox.

Instructor Reflection

To best prepare for this lesson, consider how you and your students have incorporated *Strong Start* skills into daily classroom activities. Think about how you model emotion language and coping skills. Consider how you give students feedback on their use of language and skills. Consider emphasizing particular skills or areas in which your students need the most review.

Preparation

The Finishing UP! lesson consists of a review of the major concepts presented in this curriculum. It may be helpful to review previous lessons prior to presenting this lesson. The following is an outline of topics covered.

Understanding Your Feelings 1 and 2

- Review Supplement 10.2, which shows the six basic feelings.
- Identify feelings as those that feel good and not so good on the inside.
- Identify okay and not okay ways of showing feelings.

When You're Angry

- Review Supplement 10.3, which shows the Stop, Count, In, Out strategy.
- Identify how our bodies feel when we are angry.
- Identify synonyms for *anger*.
- Identify situations when we might feel angry.
- Review Ways that Help and Ways that Hurt in handling anger.

When You're Happy

- Identify how our bodies feel when we are happy.
- Identify synonyms for *happy*.
- Learn the concept of Happy Talk.

When You're Worried

- Identify how our bodies feel when we are worried.
- Identify synonyms for the word *worry*.
- Identify how Happy Talk and the Stop, Count, In, Out strategy can help us when we are worried.
- Learn a relaxation strategy for keeping a calm body.

Understanding Other People's Feelings

- Review Supplement 10.2, which shows the six basic feelings.
- Identify physical cues to understand how someone else is feeling.

Being a Good Friend

- Identify nice voices and not nice voices.
- Identify listening skills: eye contact and body language.
- Learn about making and keeping friends.

Solving People Problems

- Review the Stop, Count, In, Out strategy.
- Review Happy Talk.
- Review how to be a friend.
- Identify how to fix problems.

Introduction

 10 MINS. Communicate the lesson's purpose and objectives clearly. Explain to students that they will complete the final lesson of the *Strong Start—Pre-K* curriculum. Tell them that topics they have been covering for the past few weeks will be reviewed. Point out that they have learned many skills during these lessons that are vital to their social and emotional health, and they will have opportunities to use these skills throughout their lives.

Optional Focusing Activity

Sample Script

Before we get started with our Strong Start lesson for today, let's get calm and focused. Sit up straight and close your eyes. Take five deep balloon breaths.

Today, we are going to complete a special class called Strong Start. In this class, we learned with a special friend. His name is Henry. In this class, Henry helped us understand our feelings and other people's feelings. He also helped us learn about being a good friend. He is a special part of our class. Even though this is our last lesson, Henry will continue to be with us. Every time we met over the last several weeks, we did special exercises. We didn't run outside or lift big, heavy weights. During the Feelings Exercise Group, we worked on growing strong on the inside instead of on the outside. Everyone needs to be healthy—on the inside and on the outside. This class helped us to be healthy on the inside and in the way we work and play with other people.

Use Supplement 10.1 to review the topics covered in *Strong Start—Pre-K*.

Sample Script

Hold up your hand if you can tell me some of the important things we learned in this class.

Point to the picture cues on Supplement 10.1 to review the following lesson topics:

- Understanding our feelings
- Understanding other people's feelings
- Feeling angry
- Feeling happy
- Feeling worried
- Being a friend
- Solving people problems

Read a Book from the Literature List

 15 MINS. Read a book from the following list of examples, or choose your own book to share with students. Think about choosing a book that will allow you to point out several of the skills learned during *Strong Start—Pre-K*. Use this portion of the lesson as an opportunity to discuss any terms or concepts that may be relevant to your class at this time, to revisit any of the ideas that need expansion, or to simplify and refresh ideas.

- *Feelings* by Aliki
- *The Way I Feel* by Janan Cain
- *Feelings* by Joanne Brisson Murphy
- *The Feelings Book* by Todd Parr
- *My Many Colored Days* by Dr. Seuss

Closure

 1 MIN. Gather your students together and review key points.

Sample Script

Today, we reviewed many things we have learned in Strong Start. We learned about our feelings and other people's feelings. We learned how to be a good friend and how to solve problems with others. Henry has been our very good friend and he has taught us so much. Now that we have completed our lessons, we need to continue to work hard to remember all that Henry has shared with us. He will continue to be a part of our classroom community and remind us of all that we have learned.

Congratulations! You have completed Strong Start and have learned how to be strong on the inside and in the way that you work and play with other people.

Extension Activity: *Strong Start* Toolbox

Purpose and Objectives

The purpose of this extension activity is to provide students with closure on *Strong Start—Pre-K* lessons and enable them to continue practice of skills.

Materials

- ☐ Shoe boxes
- ☐ Postal paper to wrap boxes
- ☐ Markers
- ☐ *Strong Start—Pre-K* activity artifacts

Procedure

1. Students decorate a *Strong Start* box or toolbox.
2. Students place items inside that they have created during curriculum implementation (e.g., sensory bags from Lesson 7) in the box.

About *Strong Start*

We learned about our feelings.

feeling *angry*   feeling *happy*   feeling *worried*

We learned about other people's feelings.

We learned about being a friend.

We learned how to relax and feel calm.

And we learned about solving problems.

Basic Feelings

Happy

Sad

Afraid

Angry

Surprised

Disgusted

The Stop, Count, In, Out Strategy

STOP		When you feel a spark, **stop** what you are doing.
COUNT	1 2 3 4 6 5 9 7 8 10	**Count** to 10.
IN		Take a deep breath **in**.
OUT		Breathe **out**.

Strong Start Bulletin

Dear Family,

Today, your child participated in the last lesson of **Strong Start—Pre-K,** a curriculum designed to boost the social and emotional development of young children. In this class, we learned with a special stuffed bear, **Henry.** Henry helped us understand our feelings and other people's feelings. He also helped us learn about being a good friend. He is a special part of our class. Even though this was our last lesson, Henry will continue to be with us in class and serve as a reminder of all that we have learned. During our lessons over the last several weeks, we engaged in activities and discussions that will encourage your child to work on being **healthy** on the inside as well as on the outside.

Strong Start helped your child:

To learn about our
feelings

To learn about other
people's feelings

To learn about
being a friend

To learn about
solving problems

And to learn how to relax
and feel calm

Although the lessons of **Strong Start** have been completed, please continue to encourage your child to use the skills and strategies presented in class and in the bulletins sent home. Together, we can continue to support your child's social and emotional health. Thank you!

Fidelity Checklist

I. Introduction

☐ Explain that this is the final *Strong Start* lesson and it will be a review of previous lessons.

☐ Point out that the skills students have learned are vital to social-emotional health (healthy on the inside).

☐ Question students on the skills they have learned.

☐ Use Supplement 10.3 picture cues to review topics.

II. Read a Book from the Literature List

Book Title/Author: _____

☐ Use relevant questions to guide the discussion.

III. Closure

☐ Provide a quick overview of what has been learned.

☐ Encourage students to work hard to remember skills/lessons they have learned.

SECTION III

Appendices

Appendices

Strong Start Booster Lesson 1

SEL Competencies Addressed in This Lesson

Teacher Notes

Purpose and Objectives

The purpose of this lesson is to review *Strong Start—Pre-K* Lessons 1–5.

- Students will review the purpose of the *Strong Start—Pre-K* curriculum.

- Students will name feelings and describe okay and not okay ways of expressing feelings.

- Students will review how to use physical cues to understand how someone else is feeling.

- Students will review the concept that different people have different feelings in the same situation.

- Students will review Happy Talk and the Stop, Count, In, Out strategy.

Materials Needed

- ☐ Henry (stuffed animal mascot)

- ☐ Supplement 1.1 (laminated card)

- ☐ Supplements 2.1–2.6 (feelings pictures on laminated cards)

- ☐ Supplement 4.3 (laminated card)

- ☐ An envelope for each student

- ☐ Enough copies of Basic Feelings Cards (Supplement A.1) for each student

- ☐ Enough *Strong Start* Feelings Bingo Cards (Supplement A.2) for each student

- ☐ Bingo Spinner (Supplement A.3)

☐ Bingo markers

☐ Paper plates, brads, scissors, and crayons

☐ A book from the literature list in Appendix C (or one of your choice)

Running Short on Time?

Consider segmenting the lesson. You may choose to split up the review activities as you see fit.

Instructor Reflection

To best prepare for this lesson, consider how you and your students have incorporated Strong Start skills into daily classroom activities since you completed the program. Think about how you model emotion language and coping skills. Consider how you give students feedback on their use of language and skills. Consider emphasizing particular skills or areas in which your students need the most review. Have students been incorporating skills learned regularly?

Preparation

The first booster lesson consists of a review of the major concepts presented in Lessons 1–5 of this curriculum. It may be helpful to flip back through these lessons before presenting this lesson. This might also be an appropriate time to focus on content that students have not yet mastered. Be sure to choose a book from the literature list (Appendix C) that addresses the needs of your class.

Introduction

 1 MIN.

Communicate clearly the lesson's purpose and objectives. Explain to your students that topics from the *Strong Start* curriculum will be reviewed. Tell them that it is always important to review the many skills previously introduced because they are vital to social and emotional health, and students will have opportunities to use these skills throughout their lives. Use Supplement 1.1 (from Lesson 1).

Optional Focusing Activity

Sample Script

Before we get started with our Strong Start lesson for today, let's get calm and focused. Sit up straight and close your eyes. Take five deep balloon breaths.

Sample Script

Today, we are going to take time to remember a special class called Strong Start. In this class, we learned with a special friend. Henry has been with us since we began Strong Start, and he has helped us to understand our feelings and other people's feelings. He has also helped us to learn about being a good friend. He is a special part of our class. Each week, when we participated in Strong Start lessons, we completed special exercises. We didn't run outside or lift big, heavy weights. We worked on growing strong on the inside during the Feelings Exercise Group. Everyone needs to be healthy—on the inside and on the outside. This class helped us to learn how to be healthy on the inside for our whole lives.

Review of Topics

🕐 20 MINS. Explain that a large part of *Strong Start* had to do with naming feelings and handling our feelings. Use the following script as a guide for your discussion.

Sample Script

The lessons that we learned a long time ago included giving names to our feelings. It is important to know how to name our feelings because it helps us to tell others how we are feeling on the inside. When we can tell others how we are feeling, it may seem easier to be good friends and to solve problems.

Use the following ideas and activities to guide your discussion.

1. Understanding your feelings

    - Display and review Supplements 2.1–2.6 (from Lesson 2), which show the six basic feelings.

    - Remind students that it is okay to have any feeling and that many people will have different feelings in the same situation. This is also an appropriate time to discuss that some people might be feeling more than one feeling at once (e.g., I was surprised and happy when I arrived at my surprise birthday party).

    - Consider engaging in an activity at a later time that allows students to label feelings and determine which are good and not so good feelings. Examples of activities frequently used are included in the Additional Activities section. Encourage students to give synonyms for various feelings and to identify how their bodies feel when they are experiencing an emotion.

2. Okay and not okay ways to handle feelings

    - Remind students that there are okay and not okay ways of showing feelings.

3. Understanding other people's feelings

    - Display and review Supplements 4.1–4.6 (from Lesson 4), which show the six basic feelings.

Situation	How Henry looks and feels
During recess, Henry's teacher tells the class that they are going to learn a new game.	Henry smiles and jumps up and down. He is *happy* because he loves new games.
Fish sticks are served for lunch at school.	Henry turns his head away and scrunches up his nose. He is *disgusted* because he does not like to eat fish sticks.
The wind is blowing, and there is a loud crack of thunder.	Henry jumps and then hides his head under his pillow. He is *scared*.
Henry's best friend is going to a new school.	Henry hangs his head, and a tear drips from his eye. He is *sad* that his friend is leaving.
Henry walks in the front door and finds his mom has baked cookies.	He smiles and runs to his mom and says, "I didn't know you were making cookies today!" He is *surprised*.
Henry's baby sister chewed on his favorite toy.	Henry turns red in the face and clenches his fists. He is *angry*.

- Remind students that it is okay to have any feeling and that many people will have different feelings in the same situation.

- Use the above examples of Henry's feelings to help children better understand how different children may have different feelings in the same situation.

4. Angry

- Display Supplement 5.3 (from Lesson 5), The Stop, Count, In, Out strategy.

- Identify situations in which we might feel angry.

- Play Stand Up, Sit Down with the following examples to remind children of Ways that Help and Ways that Hurt in handling anger.

Spark	What Henry does	Is it a Way that Helps or a Way that Hurts?
Henry's friends say that he can't play in the dramatic play area.	Henry yells, "I'll never be your friend again!"	It's a Way that Hurts.
Henry's friends say that he can't play in the dramatic play area.	Henry takes a deep breath and counts to 10 before asking the teacher for help.	It's a Way that Helps.

Read a Book from the Literature List

⏲ 10 MINS.   Choose a book from the literature list (Appendix C) that includes concepts relevant to your class at this time. Use the book as a forum for further discussion. Consider how characters in the story are feeling, how they handle their feelings, or how they recognize the feelings of others.

Closure

⏲ 1 MIN.   Gather your students together and review key points.

Sample Script

Today, we reviewed much of what we learned in Strong Start. We reviewed how to label our feelings, and we discussed okay and not okay ways to handle our feelings. We also talked about understanding how other people feel. Henry has helped us to remember these important skills, and he will continue to do so. Next time we meet, we will talk more about being a good friend and solving problems with others.

Additional Activities

⏲ 10 MINS.   ***Complete one or more of these activities within 2 days of lesson implementation.***

Paper Plate Faces: Have students decorate paper plates that look like themselves. Give students brads, and have them fasten smiles, frowns, and so forth to the mouth portion. Ask students to practice using the paper plate to show different feelings.

Feelings Envelope: Have students cut the six basic feelings from Supplement A.1 and place them in an envelope. Have them pull out the feeling they are experiencing.

Feelings Bingo: Use the Bingo Cards (Supplement A.2) to play a developmentally appropriate game of bingo. In preparation for bingo, use Supplement A.3 to create a bingo spinner. Fasten the spinner arrow to the center of the circle with a brad. Encourage children to take turns using the bingo spinner. Have children place a marker on the feeling on their bingo board that matches the feeling the spinner is pointing to. Have children try to cover their entire boards with markers.

Basic Feelings Cards

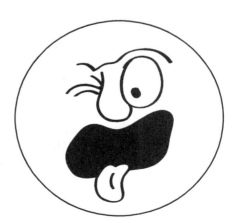

Strong Start Feelings Bingo

Bingo Spinner

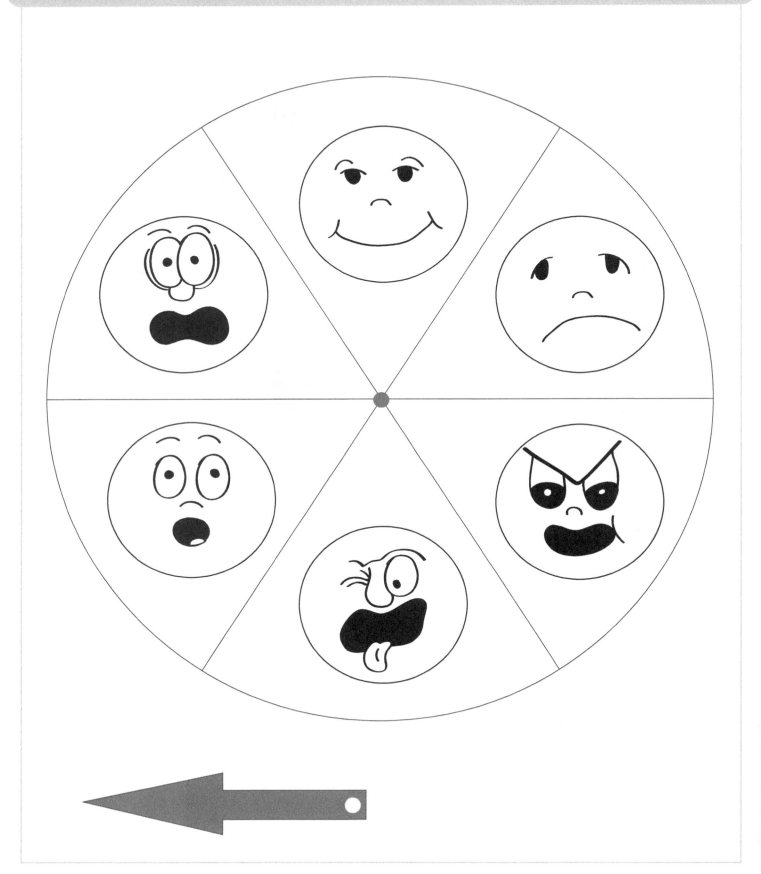

APPENDIX
B

Strong Start Booster Lesson 2

SEL Competencies Addressed in This Lesson

Responsible decision making · Self-awareness · Self-management · Social awareness · Relationship skills

Teacher Notes

_____

_____

_____

_____

_____

_____

_____

_____

Purpose and Objectives

The purpose of this lesson is to review *Strong Start—Pre-K* Lessons 6–9.

- Students will review the concept of Happy Talk.
- Students will review how good friends use eyes, ears, and bodies to show caring.
- Students will review problem-solving strategies.

Materials Needed

☐ Henry (stuffed animal mascot)

☐ Supplements 2.1–2.6 (laminated cards)

☐ Supplement 7.2 (laminated card)

☐ Supplement 9.1 (laminated card)

☐ Class book developed during Lesson 8 (Being a Good Friend)

☐ A book from the literature list in Appendix C (or one of your choice)

Running Short on Time?

Consider segmenting the lesson. You may choose to split up the review activities as you see fit.

Instructor Reflection

To best prepare for this lesson, consider how you and your students have incorporated Strong Start skills into daily classroom activities since you completed the program. Think about how you model emotion language and coping skills. Consider how you give students feedback on their use of language and skills. Consider emphasizing particular skills or areas in which your students need the most review. Have students been incorporating skills learned regularly?

Preparation

The second booster lesson consists of a review of the major concepts presented in Lessons 6–9 of this curriculum. It may be helpful to flip back through these lessons before presenting this lesson. This might also be an appropriate time to focus on content that students have not yet mastered. Be sure to choose a book from the literature list that addresses the needs of your class.

Introduction

🕐 1 MIN.

Communicate clearly the lesson's purpose and objectives. Explain to your students that topics from the *Strong Start* curriculum will be reviewed. Remind your students that it is always important to review the many skills introduced previously because they are vital to social and emotional health, and students will have opportunities to use these skills throughout their lives.

To activate prior knowledge, review and discuss topics and main ideas from Booster Lesson 1 (Appendix A). Make sure to refer to naming feelings and identifying those feelings that are good and not so good. Have students give examples of okay and not okay ways of showing feelings, especially the Stop, Count, In, Out strategy. Use Supplements 2.1–2.6 (from Lesson 2).

Optional Focusing Activity

Sample Script

Before we get started with our Strong Start lesson for today, let's get calm and focused. Sit up straight and close your eyes. Take five deep balloon breaths.

During our last meeting, we discussed how to name our feelings. We talked about what our bodies look like when we are experiencing a feeling, how to understand other people's feelings, and what we do to handle our feelings. Raise your hand if you can tell me an important idea we learned during that lesson.

Today, we are going to continue to remember a special class called Strong Start. Henry will be with us and will help us to remember Happy Talk, how to be a good friend, and how to solve problems.

Review of Topics

⏲ 25 MINS. Explain that a large part of *Strong Start* had to do with looking at the faces and bodies of others to understand how they are feeling. Another important part of *Strong Start* included thinking about how we use our bodies to show that we are good friends and problem solvers.

Sample Script

The lessons that we learned a long time ago asked us to be detectives and search for clues to help us figure out how other people are feeling. We learned to pay attention to the faces and bodies of the people around us. Being detectives makes it easier for us to make friends and solve problems.

Use the following ideas and activities to guide your discussion.

1. Happy

    - Remind children about the concept of Happy Talk.

    - Play Stand Up, Sit Down with the following examples to help students review Happy Talk.

Problem	What Henry says to himself	Is Henry using Happy Talk?
Henry's friends say that he can't play in the dramatic play area.	"They never let me play! I'll never play with them again."	No
Henry's friends say that he can't play in the dramatic play area.	"I am mad, and I think I need the teacher to help me fix this."	Yes

2. Worry

    - Review how Happy Talk and the Stop, Count, In, Out strategy can help us when we are worried. Use Supplement 7.2 (from Lesson 7).

    - Review how to keep a calm body.

    - Act out the following scenario with Henry to review how Henry uses Happy Talk to handle his worries. Add any examples that seem particularly relevant to your class.

        Henry: "My teacher is not here today because she is sick. There is a new teacher. What if she doesn't know the rules? What if she forgets to hand out the snacks? What if she doesn't know that we don't turn all the lights off at rest time?"

        Henry: [Henry counts to 10 and takes a deep breath. He approaches the substitute teacher.] "I am a little scared because my teacher is not here today and maybe you don't know how things work."

> *Substitute teacher:* "Well, Henry. Thanks for being brave and naming your feeling. Maybe you can help me remember how things are supposed to go."

3. Being a good friend

   - Remind students that good friends use nice voices and use eyes, ears, and calm bodies when listening to others.

   - Review how good friends take notice and care. Consider engaging in the additional activity presented at the end of this lesson.

4. Solving people problems

   - Review strategies for solving problems. Remind students to use a Way that Helps in handling anger and to use Happy Talk.

   - Review the following concepts that help when trying to make a problem better.

     Use the Stop, Count, In, Out strategy (Supplement 9.1 from Lesson 9).

     Use Happy Talk.

     Be a friend.

     Make it better.

     Emphasize that solving problems involves helping all parties to feel better.

   - Engage in a sharing activity. Have students think about times when they have had problems (e.g., arguing over toys, not taking turns, working together). Encourage students to consider whether or not they effectively problem-solved the situation.

   - Ensure respectful sharing by reminding students not to use names and to remember to use nice words.

Read a Book from the Literature List

🕐 10 MINS. Choose a book from the literature list (Appendix C) that includes concepts relevant to your class at this time. Use the book as a forum for further discussion. Consider how characters in the story are feeling, how they handle their feelings, or how they recognize the feelings of others.

Closure

🕐 1 MIN. Gather your students together and review key points.

Sample Script

Today, we reviewed much of what we learned in Strong Start. We reviewed how to be detectives and look for body clues so that we know how others are feeling.

We remembered how to be good friends and problem solvers. Henry has helped us to remember these important skills. He has been our very good friend and has taught us so much. Now that we have completed our review lessons, we need to continue to work hard to remember all that Henry has shared with us. He will continue to be a part of our classroom community and remind us of all that we have learned.

Additional Activity: Class Book

🕐 10 MINS. ***Complete this activity within 2 days of lesson implementation.***

If your class compiled a class book during Lesson 8, read it aloud to the class. Consider adding new ideas based on what children have learned over time.

Recommended *Strong Start—Pre-K* Literature List

LESSON 1: THE FEELINGS EXERCISE GROUP

- *Feelings* by Aliki
- *The Way I Feel* by Janan Cain
- *Feelings* by Joanne Brisson Murphy
- *The Feelings Book* by Todd Parr
- *My Many Colored Days* by Dr. Seuss

LESSON 2: UNDERSTANDING YOUR FEELINGS 1

- *Everybody Has Feelings/Todos Tenemos Sentimientos: The Moods of Children* by Charles E. Avery
- *My First Day at Nursery School* by Becky Edwards
- *How Are You Peeling? Foods with Moods* by Saxton Freymann and Joost Elffers
- *On Monday When It Rained* by Cherryl Kachenmeister
- *My Many Colored Days* by Dr. Seuss

LESSON 3: UNDERSTANDING YOUR FEELINGS 2

- *The Chocolate-Covered-Cookie Tantrum* by Deborah Blumenthal
- *The Way I Feel* by Janan Cain
- *The Feelings Book* by Todd Parr
- *Lots of Feelings* by Shelley Rotner
- *Sometimes I Like to Cry* by Elizabeth Stanton and Henry B. Stanton

LESSON 4: UNDERSTANDING OTHER PEOPLE'S FEELINGS

- *Harriet, You'll Drive Me Wild* by Mem Fox
- *Frog in the Middle* by Susanna Gretz
- *Chrysanthemum* by Kevin Henkes
- *The Rat and the Tiger* by Keiko Kasza
- *I Love My New Toy!* by Mo Willems

LESSON 5: WHEN YOU'RE ANGRY

- *The Anger Monster* by Jennifer Anzin
- *When Sophie Gets Angry—Really, Really Angry...* by Molly Bang
- *Josh's Smiley Faces: A Story About Anger* by Gina Ditta-Donahue
- *Just Being Me #1: I'm SO Mad!* by Robie H. Harris
- *Sometimes I'm Bombaloo* by Rachel Vail

LESSON 6: WHEN YOU'RE HAPPY

- *I Like Myself!* by Karen Beaumont
- *Fun Is a Feeling* by Chara M. Curtis
- *Stand Tall, Molly Lou Melon!* by Patty Lovell
- *Beautiful Oops!* by Barney Saltzberg
- *Super-Completely and Totally the Messiest* by Judith Viorst

LESSON 7: WHEN YOU'RE WORRIED

- *Even if I Did Something Awful* by Barbara Shook Hazen
- *Wemberly Worried* by Kevin Henkes
- *The Kissing Hand* by Audrey Penn
- *The Good-Bye Book* by Judith Viorst
- *Owl Babies* by Martin Waddell

LESSON 8: BEING A GOOD FRIEND

- *We Are Best Friends* by Aliki
- *Do You Want to Be My Friend?* by Eric Carle
- *How to Grow a Friend* by Sara Gillingham
- *Enemy Pie* by Derek Munson
- *Yo! Yes?* by Chris Raschka

LESSON 9: SOLVING PEOPLE PROBLEMS

- *Move Over, Twerp* by Martha Alexander
- *I Can't Wait* by Elizabeth Crary
- *I'm Frustrated* by Elizabeth Crary
- *Bet You Can't* by Penny Dale
- *Chester's Way* by Kevin Henkes
- *Words Are Not for Hurting* by Elizabeth Verdick and Marieka Heinlen

LESSON 10: FINISHING UP!

- *Feelings* by Aliki
- *The Way I Feel* by Janan Cain
- *Feelings* by Joanne Brisson Murphy
- *The Feelings Book* by Todd Parr
- *My Many Colored Days* by Dr. Seuss